PASSPORT NOT REQUIRED

U.S. Volunteers in the Royal Navy, 1939–1941

Eric Dietrich-Berryman, Charlotte Hammond, and R. E. White

NAVAL INSTITUTE PRESS
Annapolis, Maryland

Naval Institute Press
291 Wood Road
Annapolis, MD 21402

Library of Congress Cataloging-in-Publication Data
Dietrich-Berryman, Eric.
Passport not required : U.S. volunteers in the Royal Navy, 1939-1941 / Eric Dietrich-Berryman, Charlotte Hammond, and R. E. White.
p. cm.
Includes bibliographical references and index.
ISBN 978-1-59114-224-9 (acid-free paper) 1. Great Britain. Royal Navy—History—World War, 1939-1945. 2. Americans—Great Britain—History—20th century. 3. World War, 1939-1945—Naval operations, British. 4. Sailors—United States—Biography. I. Hammond, Charlotte, 1967- II. White, R. E. (Ronald E.), 1937- III. Title.
D770.D46 2010
940.54'5941092313—dc22

2010022000

Printed in the United States of America on acid-free paper

14 13 12 11 10 9 8 7 6 5 4 3 2
First printing

In Memory of Police Constable R. E. White, Sussex Constabulary
Sailor, Scholar, Cross-Country Hiker
and Friend

CONTENTS

FIGURES

FOREWORD

H.R.H. Prince Michael of Kent, GCVO, Honorary Rear Admiral, Royal Naval Reserve. (Permission of H.R.H. Prince Michael)

I am delighted to write a foreword to *Passport Not Required: U.S. Volunteers in the Royal Navy, 1939–1941*. The story tells of a number of gallant Americans who, when the fate of Britain and of the cause of freedom hung in the balance, volunteered to serve in the Royal Navy in the period 1939–41, before America's entry into the conflict. Their numbers may not have been great, but the fact that they came at a moment when Britain stood alone meant so much. No man can do more for another country than to volunteer to fight for it.

Two special remembrance services took place, in 2001 and 2004, at the Old Royal Naval College, Greenwich. Most of the American volunteers were initially trained there and, to honour the twenty-two identified at that time, their names were inscribed, with due ceremony, on memorial tablets in the Painted Hall of the College. Colours of the Royal Navy and of the United States are permanently displayed with the tablets as a mark of respect.

Services like these are a fitting tribute and demonstrate in the finest possible way the special relationship between the United Kingdom and the United States. The courage and fortitude shown by these American volunteers, who came over to Britain at such a dangerous time, leaving the safety of their own homes and country, are an example to us all.

I am extremely proud of my connection with the Royal Naval Reserve and the professionalism of its people. The story of these twenty-two American volunteers to the Royal Naval Reserve is a gallant one that should never be forgotten.

H.R.H. Prince Michael of Kent, GCVO
Honorary Rear Admiral, Royal Naval Reserve

Note: President Franklin D. Roosevelt is one of Prince Michael's godfathers.

ACKNOWLEDGMENTS

In gratitude for their assistance in compiling this book: Rear Admiral Draper Kauffman, Francis Stanley Parker, William Perkins Homans, Edwin Fairman Russell, and David Gibson. It is a grace to have known such men. Our thanks also to family members and friends of the RNVR volunteers who spoke with us and who provided contacts, documents, and photographs: Daphne Abeel, Serena Churchill Balfour, Emily Morison Beck, Cameron Beck, Frances Berges, Allen Bigelow, Elizabeth Kauffman Bush, Richard Cherry, Winston Spencer Churchill, Charles Collins, Beryl Crane, Ann Davenport Dixon, Thelma Fabian, Iva Ferris, Kathleen Ferris, Noel Ferris, Wilfred Ferris, Kathleen Franklin-Collins, Sheila Fuse, Eric Gibson, John Peter Hayes, George Hoague, Lydia Hoague, James Homans, Peter Homans, William Homans, Draper Kauffman Jr., Kelsey Kauffman, Edmund "Skip" Kittredge, Rolf Konow, Ida Kraft, Derek A. Lee, Rigby Lee, Elizabeth Homans McKenna, Samuel Loring Morison, Jim Paul, Diantha Parker, Judy Parker, Lucy Parker, Michael and Laura Sabatell, Andrew Stilwell, Peter Stilwell, Roger Stilwell, and John Wallace.

Scholars and officials who gave their support: Davis Ashby, Naval Historical Branch; Admiral of the Fleet Sir Benjamin Bathurst; Vice Admiral Sir Jeremy Blackham; Rear Admiral Joseph Leslie Blackham; Evelyn Cherpak, U.S. Naval Institute; Admiral Roy Clare, director National Maritime Museum; Captain I. F. Corder; Emma Crocker, curator of photographs, Imperial War Museum; Captain Prentice Cushing Jr.; Bill Dawes; Allison Duffield, Department of Printed Books, Imperial War Museum; Alan Giddings; Sir Phillip Goodhart; Marilyn Gurney, Harvard University Archives; Professor John

Hattendorff, Naval War College; Dr. Hans-Georg Hess; James Hessman, editor emeritus, *Seapower* magazine; Nick Hewitt, Imperial War Museum; Henry Higgs; Rear Admiral J. R. Hill; Mark Kahn, Smithsonian Institution, National Air & Space Museum; Debbie Ketchum; Renee Klish, art curator, U.S. Army Center of Military History; Admiral of the Fleet Lord Terry Lewin, KG; The Honourable Timothy Lewin; Captain James Mader; Mary Moran; Lincoln Paine; Charles Pellegrini, U.S. National Archives & Records Administration; Commander John Prichard, The Naval Club; Ken Reed and David R. Schwartz, Smithsonian Institution, National Air & Space Museum; Rear Admiral James R. Stark; Sir Harold Walker; and Richard Woodman.

Colonel Kieran O'Kelly (British English) and Briana Easter (American English) proofread the draft with skill and attention to detail; Timothy Foote, a wonderfully literate former editor at *Time* and the *Smithsonian Magazine* brought common sense to the structure of the prose; David Poyer turned away from his enthralling sea yarns to go through the first draft line by line; Eric Gibson organized the information and gave it coherence and rallied us during bleak times; Kimberly B. Rotter, Bill and Jo Clark, Karen Truckey—our gifted designer—and Sarah Truckey researched for us at the National Records Office in St. Louis; Professor William C. Truckey, a meticulous grammarian, saved us from sounding like country dolts; John Iler, Fr. John Hilary Hayden, OSB, put aside his writings on liturgical music to help with sense and structure; and Roberta Berryman gave encouragement and abundant good humor.

INTRODUCTION

In recent years, it has become somewhat fashionable for writers and broadcasters, understandably anxious to ensure that their work reaches as wide an audience as possible, to attach labels like "secret" or "forgotten" to their work, or to refer to every story as an "untold" one. While forgivable, the knock-on effect of such slapdash use of these terms has been rather to devalue them. Yet every so often a genuinely untold story, a real piece of "forgotten" history, does come to light, and the subject of *Passport Not Required* is unequivocally one of them.

This extraordinary narrative leaps back from the unveiling of a memorial in the Old Royal Naval College's beautiful Painted Hall in October 2001, to a time when a handful of men came from the other side of the Atlantic to stand with Britain in her time of greatest peril. The Americans who served with the Royal Air Force's "Eagle Squadrons" have been celebrated in narrative and on screen many times over the years, and have their own memorial in Grosvenor Square, but the story of those who served with the Royal Navy has, until now, remained obscure.

What drives a person to go and fight in someone else's war? The subject is a source of endless fascination, and in the twenty-two men whose stories are told in these pages, a whole range of motives can be found, from the touching Anglophilia of Alex Cherry to the striking idealism of Bill Homans. A restless spirit of adventure, an inability to settle, a visceral loathing of Nazism and what it stood for—all played their part in sending these twenty-two men, not always so very young, across the Atlantic to Britain in her hour of dire need.

But *Passport Not Required* is not just a tale of men at war, and a very good one. It also reflects the extraordinary efforts made by a small group of people to ensure that this story be released and the twenty-two men be allowed to take their places in the vast saga of World War II. Particular credit is due to the remarkable Ronald "Chalky" White, who gave up the last years of his life to this project; his co-researcher Charlotte Hammond; and Eric Berryman, who stepped up to write the book and ensure that others could benefit from Chalky and Charlotte's detective work. This book stands not just as a testament to those twenty-two resolute men who came to Britain to fight in 1939–41, but also to those who struggled with much determination to make sure the volunteers would be remembered. It is a notable achievement, and proof that those of us bearing the word "historian" in our job titles are only just the privileged tip of a very large iceberg.

Nick Hewitt, MA
Naval Historian
Imperial War Museum, London

ACRONYMS

ASDIC	Early version of, predecessor of, sonar. ASDIC, deliberate nonsense invented by the British for security reasons, signifies antisubmarine detection investigation committee.
AVG	American Volunteer Group
CB	Companion of the Most Honourable Order of the Bath. This award ranks just below a knighthood.
CVO	Commander of the Royal Victorian Order. Awarded for personal service to the monarch.
DD	destroyer
DFC and bar	Distinguished Flying Cross. Bar indicates subsequent award of same decoration.
DSC	Distinguished Service Cross
DSO	Distinguished Service Order
EOD	Explosive Ordnance Disposal
GCVO	Knight Grand Cross of the Victorian Order
HM	His Majesty
LST	Landing Ship Tank
HMCS	His Majesty's Canadian Ship
ML	Motor Launch
HMS	His Majesty's Ship
HMT	His Majesty's Transport
KCB	Knight Commander of the Most Honourable Order of the Bath

KG	The Most Honourable Order of the Garter, Britain's highest order of knighthood.
LCS	Landing Craft Support
LRCP	Licentiate of the Royal College of Physicians of London. British medical qualification.
LSE	U.S. Landing Ship, Emergency. A British designation of LSTs built in the United States and on loan to the United Kingdom.
LST	Landing Ship Tank
LVG	biplane *Luft-Verkehrs-Gesellschaft*
MRCS	Member of the Royal College of Surgeons. British medical qualification.
NCO	Noncommissioned Officer
OBE	Order of the British Empire
OSS	patrol boats
PO	petty officer
RAF	Royal Air Force
RB-1's convoy	Convoy Route number. RB designated St. Lawrence to the United Kingdom from September 1942, transfer of passenger ships to the United Kingdom.
RCAF	Royal Canadian Air Force
RCNR	Royal Canadian Naval Reserve
RN	Royal Navy
RNC	Royal Naval College
RNR	Royal Navy Reserve
RNVR	Royal Naval Volunteer Reserve

Ship designations. Slow, minimum of 7.5 knots; fast, at least 9 knots.

HX fast	(North America to UK)
SC slow	(North America to UK)
OB fast	(UK to North America)
ON fast	(UK to North America)
ONS slow	(UK to North America)
OT fast	(U.S. to Africa)
TO fast	(Africa to U.S.)

CU fast	(Caribbean to UK)
UC fast	(UK to Caribbean)
TM fast	(Trinidad to Gibraltar)
SS	Steam Ship
USMC	United States Marine Corps
USN	United States Navy
USNI	U.S. Naval Institute
USNR	U.S. Naval Reserve
USS LCS (L)	Landing Craft, Infantry, Large
UXB	Unexploded Bomb
VC	Victoria Cross, Britain's highest decoration for bravery in battle.
WAAC	Women's Army Auxiliary Corps
WAAF	Women's Auxiliary Air Force
WRNS	Women's Royal Naval Service

1 A Tremendous Flame Shot Upward

On October 15, 1941, HMS *Broadwater,* under command of Lieutenant Commander William M. L. Astwood, RN, received orders to assist a convoy. The fifty ships he was sent to protect had been designated SC-48 (SC meant slow). They headed east into the open ocean bound from Canada for the United Kingdom. Buffeting from heavy weather further inhibited SC-48's 7.5-knot speed. The North Atlantic was well into autumn with winter already discernible in the air. Men pulled down their caps, turned up their collars, and grunted against the biting cold. Binoculars scoured the sea for signs of the enemy but human eyes were poor protection against submarines.

Lieutenant John Stanley Parker, RNVR, on *Broadwater*'s bridge watch that night had confided in a letter to his wife, "All I can say is that at long last I'm doing exactly what I was made for, in what I have always wanted . . . doing what has to be done and all I'm fit for any more. Am absolutely fit, tired and happy. I'm learning all the time—every hour something. But it is not diagrams on a blackboard. If only I could tell you what I've heard and seen. . . . It's a queer sensation this life. It is as if I've always lived this way . . . and as if I were to always so live" (Judith Parker papers). There was not much time for thoughts of home when he took his turn to conn the ship. Wind force and slowness made the convoy a prime wolf pack target. Early in the morning two days later Astwood successfully attacked *U-432* and was granted credit for a probable sinking. The cheers did not last long. *Broadwater* herself became a fatality when a torpedo from *U-101* (*Kapitänleutnant* Ernst Mengersen) slammed into the hull. The detonation blew away the upper bridge works and bow, making the British ship an unsalvageable hulk. On bridge watch again was Lieutenant Parker.

HMS *Broadwater* (ex–USS *Mason* DD-191) was one of the fleet of overage warships turned over by the United States to Britain in 1941 in exchange for century leases on strategic bases in the Western Hemisphere. At Halifax the ship was commissioned into the Third [Town Class] Flotilla, Newfoundland Escort Force and renamed in honor of the towns of that name in Sussex, England, and Hog Island, Virginia. Town Class refers to the Admiralty renaming Lend-Lease ships after towns common to the United States and Britain. The College of Arms began a design for the ship's badge that included storm clouds and rain, symbols that indicated the college knew the American *Broadwater* had suffered in the great nor'easter of August 23, 1933, when the Atlantic met the Chesapeake Bay in nine-foot tidal surges that battered and made unrecognizable virtually every built structure in the village. By the time USS *Mason* changed her name and nationality, the Broadwater, Virginia, post office had closed, leaving only two stubborn old residents amid the wreckage and broken foundations of what had been a thriving community, much of which now lay drowned. The ship's heraldic badge was discarded when the ship was lost.

HMS *Broadwater* played her role against a vastly complicated Anglo-American backdrop. Before the Japanese attack on Pearl Harbor many people in the United States tilted in favor of supporting England. There was equally passionate opposition by "America First" isolationists who wanted no part of Europe's latest scrape. The occupant of the White House leaned heavily toward Britain. Franklin Roosevelt's definition of neutrality was unmistakably, energetically pro-British. Accordingly, the U.S. Navy was dispatched to accompany convoys from the Western Ocean Meeting Point, south of Newfoundland, to the Mid-Ocean Meeting Point off Iceland where the merchant ships passed to Royal Navy control. Ships from the Free French Navy and the Royal Canadian Navy escorted convoys comprising upwards of a hundred vessels. The mix of ships and flags made it well nigh impossible for U-boats to distinguish between visitors and home team. A serious incident at sea affecting U.S.-German relations was only a matter of time.

Admiral Karl Dönitz, Germany's commander in chief of submarine operations, organized his wolf packs in North Atlantic sea-lanes with considerable success. Several ships were torpedoed and destroyed in convoy SC-48 between October 15 and 17, 1941. The escort group included five U.S. ships intermixed with one British, one Canadian, and one French warship. Taking advantage of how closely the escorts stuck to the convoy and their lack of radar, U-boats quickly closed to torpedo range and fired in salvoes. Ship after ship exploded, including the Flower-class corvette HMS *Gladiolus*, lost with all hands.

An eyewitness described how "a colossal flash leapt from the convoy. In a moment it resolved itself into a tremendous flame which shot upwards from the water, accompanied by a roar like the sound of a passing express train. The great column of fire, whose diameter might have been equal to the length of the ship, from whose ranks it sprang, seemed almost to reach the cloud base. The whole convoy was lit up by its brilliance" (Alan Easton, Lieutenant, RCNR, CO, HMCS *Baddeck*. Archive of the Canadian War Museum).

Cohesion collapsed. Escort warships indiscriminately fired star shells and snowflakes (startlingly bright illumination devices), blinding the lookouts by erasing their night vision. This made it even easier for U-boat captains to sight more targets. Swinging out to avoid a Canadian corvette, USS *Kearny* (Lieutenant Commander Anthony L. Danis) made his ship a perfect target. At ten minutes past midnight a torpedo fired by *U-568* (*Kapitänleutnant* Joachim Preuss) struck the hull.

Decades later Preuss said, "As far as the U.S. destroyer *Kearny* is concerned I may mention that I did not intend to attack that vessel in the first place, which I did not recognize as being a U.S. one. I was running [on the surface] from the rear end of the convoy to the head at high speed. I had seen some big ships sailing at the head of the convoy. However, that destroyer hindered me by crossing my path several times, so finally I decided to attack her although this would necessitate shooting all four bow torpedoes" (Preuss letter to Ronald "Chalky" White ca. 1980). [It took about half an hour to reload one torpedo tube.] Aboard the badly damaged *Kearney* eleven sailors died and twenty-two were injured, including Danis. These were the first American battle casualties of World War II.

The night of October 17–18 has a place in the annals of the U.S. Navy, as it does for naval historians of the era who mark the events of that date for their influence in profoundly shifting America's perception of the war in Europe. President Roosevelt pounced on the incident and his announcement that "this torpedo was directed at every American" resonated throughout the country. The incident came at a singularly inopportune time for Hitler because Congress was hotly engaged in debating the presidential request that the last remaining restrictions of the Neutrality Act be lifted. Roosevelt broadcast, "We have wished to avoid shooting but the shooting war has started. And history recorded who fired the first shot" (FDR radio broadcast, 27 October 1941). In Berlin Hitler responded, "I have ordered German ships not to shoot when they sight American vessels but to defend themselves when attacked. I will have any German officer court-martialed who fails to defend himself" (John Dickey, "Destroyers for Great Britain," *Sea Classics*, vol. 32, March 1999).

Broadwater's captain inspected the damage to his command. He reported:

> From the bow to the after hatch of the forward seamen's mess deck [everything] was completely gone [as well as the] structure above it which contained the wardroom and officers' cabins. The upper bridge was blown away excepting for the Hotchkiss [gun] mounting. The mast was snapped and had fallen aft and the butt end had run forward into the chart room. The front of the wheelhouse had completely gone but the wheel was still standing. On the well deck there was a bit of wreckage and the deck was buckled. A considerable amount of wreckage of the bridge and forepart of the ship was found on the gun deck. The deck abaft No. 4 funnel was badly buckled and the working of the ship at both sides at this point indicated that the ship's back was probably broken. The engines and dynamos stopped immediately on explosion of the torpedo. The . . . ship appeared to be settling very slowly . . . and water was washing over the well deck. She was badly hogged. Seeing that the chances of salvage were nil, I asked [one of the other escorts, an antisubmarine trawler] HMS *Cape Warwick* to sink her by gunfire. (Lieutenant Commander W. M. L. Astwood, RN, After action report, National Archives)

Broadwater went down at 0140 on October 18.

The attack took the lives of forty-five officers and men including fifty-one-year-old John Parker, one of the Royal Navy's oldest lieutenants. He was on the bridge when the torpedo struck forty feet below, killing him instantly. A businessman, husband, and father of two adult sons, overage by decades, there was in fact no legal obligation whatever for him to have been there at all. Parker's wife, Violet, received the customary Admiralty telegram at her home: "Deeply regret to inform you that your husband is reported killed in action." Parker had lied about his age and the Royal Navy winked at the lie and made no effort to probe. There was need of deck officers.

Among the condolence letters to Violet Parker is one from her husband's teacher at the Royal Naval College, Greenwich, Commander E. Dallas Marston, RN: "I never ceased to marvel at the magnificent spirit which prompted him to take his service with us. I'm proud to think that I came to earn his esteem, and certainly to have his friendship, and that is something that I shall always treasure for such men are rare. . . . He was desperately keen on his job and doing what he wanted to do and how he worked—he was an inspiration to all of us and made me give my very best in my small way. . . . Men like John don't just disappear, and thank God our memories of them don't either" (Judith Parker papers). Parker's school chum and cousin, Charles Curtis, wrote in a class memorial, "He died as he would have easily chosen to die, killed in action, and among the first because he was among the most gallant" (Charles P. Curtis, "John S. Parker," *Groton School Quarterly*, winter 1941).

Broadwater's position at the time of her loss remained something of an enigma until the end of the twentieth century. A board of inquiry convened at Londonderry soon after the sinking determined that the ship was at least eleven or twelve miles astern of the convoy she was sent to protect. No evidence was received to explain why. The only available information came from a Royal Navy rating, Engine Room Artificer (4th Class) Beer, who testified that no extraordinary increase or decrease of revolutions had taken place in the middle watch.

The mystery of *Broadwater*'s true position—and the reason behind it—lasted for almost sixty years. In 1998, Leicester, England, resident Robert Martin explained that as a young seaman aboard *Broadwater* he was on bridge watch and overheard the captain tell the navigating officer to let the ship drop astern in order to "get" the following U-boat. U-boat tactics included pursuing a convoy, reporting course and speed to Dönitz's headquarters in France. This tactic enabled others in the wolf pack to converge and take up attacking positions. *Broadwater*'s captain had increased the distance between himself and the convoy because he wanted to surprise and destroy his foe.

One of *Broadwater*'s stokers, Johnnie Scott, lived through the ordeal and described the experience from his perspective: "HMS *Broadwater* was not really fit to be a fighting ship," he told his family,

> and, being stokers, my fellow workers and I had many harrowing experiences in her engine room trying to keep up the steam. We were often in dock for repairs and improvements. One of my ship friends was Nobby Hunt, who I'll never forget. I remember the night before we were torpedoed, he told me he had done his twenty-two years and would soon be receiving his pension. Unfortunately, he never lived to see it. Lieutenant Parker also comes to mind . . . a brave man and a volunteer. We left Newfoundland for the Clyde, and on to convoy duty. There were ships everywhere. On the fateful night of 18th October, *Broadwater* was quite far astern. The crew had appealed to the captain, Lieutenant Commander Astwood, to slow down and stop to pick up floating survivors. The men were in the oily water, screaming for their lives and shouting to be saved. The captain, I remember, came down from the bridge. He was not supposed to stop under any circumstances, but he did, and he said, "You stokers will get me strung up!" We picked up eleven thankful and exhausted young men.
>
> On hearing the Scottish accents, one of them shouted, "Good old Rangers!" and with a Glasgow sense of humor, Alex Robertson, who was my mate, replied, "Just as well you said 'Rangers' or ye'd get put back in!" Such was the comradeship of these brave men! Many other men never made it on board, as they lost their grip and slipped under the oily ship: sights I will never forget. Sadly, those eleven sailors were all killed the next night aboard *Broadwater*, along with forty-five of the ship's company. Our own men gave up their bunks in the Seamen's Mess so they could rest up. I had offered a sailor my bunk, aft (it would be warm there), but he declined, and went to sleep near his pal, resulting in his death. At about three or four in the morning, I was on the middle watch, tied onto a make-shift stool (2 pipes tied together and a strip of sheeting). The seas were very heavy and the old ship was rolling badly.
>
> Suddenly there were two bangs, a tremendous force, and *Broadwater* shuddered alarmingly. I was thrown off the stool by the impact. Jimmy

Beer, who was Fourth Eng. [*sic*] Officer said, "Go up and find out what's happened, Johnnie." So I went up to find men running everywhere and someone shouting "Abandon ship! Abandon ship!" (I think it could have been the Coxwain.) I realised with horror that the bridge had been blown away [where Lieutenant Parker had been standing watch] and the bow of *Broadwater* was gone. Men were trying, with great difficulty, to get Carley floats (dinghies) onto the water. Our lives were certainly on the line! With great speed I ran back to warn Jimmy Beer who was trying to get through to the bridge to get out. C. S. Pickering, our Chief Engineer, ordered the safety valves to be opened. He had been torpedoed before, on HMS *Curlew*, and knew that this would prevent the boilers exploding. I then made for the Carley float. Suddenly it was stuck on the screws of the propellers, as they were out of the water by this time, although the ship still seemed to be floating. I then remembered my Burberry trench coat.

I find it hard to believe now, but I was young, and I never thought I could die. I asked the guys to wait while I went back for my coat. "No-way mate," was the chorus. "We'll be gone." I thought of Martha (Mattie) my wife. Her last words were ringing in my ears, "Don't you come back without that coat!" It was her parting gift to me and she had paid £7–10 for it, in navy-blue regulation color, from the posh Paisley's store in Glasgow. Well, Mattie was, and still is, a fiery redhead, so I ran back for my coat. All this would only have taken about one minute or so: I was fit and could move fast, and I was determined not to face her without that coat! Imagine! I got the coat, only to find the float had moved away from the ship and I had to jump, coat on my back, for dear life! What a girl Mattie must have been! She is still with me today sixty-three years on and still telling me what to do! I struggled in the water and eventually was pulled on board by my pal Alex, who nearly got lynched trying to hold out for me. Fortunately, he was the only one with a Swiss Army knife to cut the tangled rope and set the dinghy free.

We made our way as best as we could in the appalling conditions. "Ship ahoy! Ship ahoy!" went up the cry. Bearing down on us was HMS *Bulldog*, almost ramming us. She was on orders, "full steam ahead." She had got a "ping" and was to take over as Senior Escort. At last the HMS *Angle* came to our rescue. The men were all in a flat spin by now and were

> desperate to get off. For us, she was our HMS "*Angel.*" I held the scramble net, while the men scurried up the side of the "Tell-Tale Charlie," as we called these ships. They were back-up ships and knew all that was going on in the convoy. I was last on and last off. The first thing I did on board *Angel* was to go down to the engine room and hang up my Burberry trench coat to dry off in the heat. We watched from our rescue ship as *Broadwater* was finished off by the gunners, and she sank in the cruel Atlantic waves, taking all the young men to the deep, including "Good old Rangers." A sad night, and a very sad sight. On reflection we should never have stopped, but they were our brothers. What would anyone have done? Our Captain must have had a kind heart.
>
> I'd love to know what happened to Jimmy Beer. I didn't see him until we reached Londonderry when he was waiting at the pier. He hugged me and said, "Thank God you're safe. Where did you go?" "Back for my coat," I replied. George Morris, the only Australian on board was also my friend. He was a big genial guy, and good company, but he too lost his life that dreadful night. No news was made public until at least a week after the event, not like today when the enemy knows every move, but I'll never forget the look on the faces that day I arrived home, wearing the Burberry trench coat! (David Scott, "A Telegram, a Trenchcoat and the Sinking of HMS *Broadwater*," BBC, *WW2 People's War*, 5 August 2005)

John Parker's death was no different from that of thousands of other men who perished in the Battle of the Atlantic, except for one fact. He was a U.S. national fighting in the armed forces of a foreign nation. The United States was not at war. By putting on another country's uniform he risked his citizenship and lost his life. Parker was the first American volunteer commissioned as a British naval officer to be killed in action in the history of the Royal Navy.

2 Twenty-two Yanks: Who Were They?

In the years before America entered the war, twenty-two citizens of the United States came to England to volunteer for the Royal Navy and serve under the White Ensign. John Parker, like the others, ignored the Neutrality Act, the law that forbade Americans from participating in the hostilities. Americans who joined the Royal Air Force's Eagle Squadron have received considerable attention, right down to contemporary times. The story of their brothers in arms, the blue and gold counterparts who went to sea in ships, never attracted much publicity and is all but unknown in both the United States and Britain.

The Americans who wore Royal Navy blue represented an assortment of occupations. Derek Lee, textiles; Charles Porter, New England real estate; Carl Konow, New York yacht broker and U.S. mail pilot; John Stilwell, theater advertising; and John Parker, sales executive and broker in Boston. There were three bankers: Edmund Kittredge from Cincinnati, and Alex Cherry and Edward Ferris from Manhattan; and a couple of medical practitioners, Oswald Deiter and Francis Hayes. Edwin Russell was a newspaper journalist and editor; Gurdan Buck, a Maryland farmer. The three youngest men were too junior to have settled into serious careers. They were romantics prospecting for adventure: David Gibson, John Leggat, and David van Epps.

By his instincts and character as well as the trajectory of his life after the war, Bill Homans was a crusader who left simply to fight a colossal evil. George Hoague was a naval architect. Only three of the volunteers had professional military backgrounds: Draper Kauffman, William Taylor, and Henry Ripley. Ripley fled from a domestic breakup, as did Peter Morison. John Hampson was a California rancher with a passion for flying. A relative described him as being a "bit of a rascal"—not necessarily a bad thing because milquetoast is not a qualification for pilots flying combat.

The men came from throughout the United States, although most of them had their roots in the Northeast where family history stretched to colonial times. The striking exception was a restless Scandinavian aristocrat who had immigrated to America. There was a sense of noblesse oblige in their actions, that privilege entails responsibility and that service tendered to a higher good was an obligation to be freely given. Like the previous generation of Americans who could not wait to join the Anglo-French alliance in World War I, volunteers from Harvard, Princeton, and Yale were predominant. For many, extensive blue-water yachting experience had contributed to an apprenticeship that was to qualify them to be accepted by Britain as seagoing naval officer candidates. Several of the men had paid for pilot lessons. Many of the volunteers had considerable disposable incomes even as the Great Depression constricted most families' ability to afford luxuries.

The economic trials of Depression era–1930s America did not affect these men in a major way. But as comfortable and safe as they were in a neutral country of their own, all of them chose to go into harm's way.

Some were wounded or injured. Two men rest with their ships on the Atlantic seabed. The volunteers showed up alone, in pairs, and in small groups. Some had in common unhappy family relationships, failed romances, or career ennui. Some had fought a "great many rounds with Old King Alcohol," and not all of them eventually retired from that sport to take "a ringside seat," as Parker said of himself (Judith Parker papers). All of them brought optimism and zeal, as well as some practical knowledge that Britain could quickly put to use fighting the Germans. Two men, William Taylor and Draper Kauffman, arrived in the earliest days of the war.

Most of the other volunteers were routed through the Royal Naval College (RNC), Greenwich, near London for training. The initial group of arrivals on June 15, 1941, made the faculty pause for a moment. These Americans were making history. Not epic history, to be sure, but something worth noting had occurred.

The college's professor of history, Geoffrey Lloyd, designed a plaque to commemorate the first three volunteers who came through the door. Though the inscription is short, almost brusque, the nobility of their action and the risk the men faced is the principal message, underscored by the plaque's special location.

About that day Lloyd wrote:

> To appreciate the position fully you must realize the political and diplomatic background obtaining at the time, at that particular moment. We were still fighting alone, the USA gradually drawing close to us but still very much uncommitted. We being tactful yet quite ready to give the States a gentle prod forwards; the USA anxious, and a trifle afraid of that prod! Here undoubtedly were three perfectly genuine citizens of the USA who were ready and anxious to throw in their lot with Great Britain. I remember we were most anxious to commemorate what seemed to be a unique occasion—as I still think it was. But it was the occasion and nothing else that we wanted to commemorate. The last thing that we wanted to do was to name the people concerned who were, I believe, doing something that was strictly against protocol if not actually against American law. (letter to Eric Berryman, circa 1976)

A few simple words sufficed: "15th June 1941 / On this day came three citizens of / the United States of America / The first of their countrymen to become Sea-Officers of / the Royal Navy." Captain John Cecil Davis, OBE, Captain of the College and Commander John Rochfort D'Oyly-Carte, Commander of the College (second in command) had the plaque set in the Painted Hall.

Finding the identity of the men who stepped forward while so many of their countrymen debated the "phony war" from a safe distance, the backgrounds from which they came, where they served, and what became of them led to the making of this book.

Parker's search for greater meaning in life began early. He was a man as restless and driven as Herman Melville's character Ishmael: "Whenever I find myself growing grim about the mouth; whenever it is a damp, drizzly November in my soul [or] from deliberately stepping into the street, and methodically knocking people's hats off—then I account it high time to get to sea as soon as I can. This is my substitute for pistol and ball . . . I quietly take to the ship."

In his youth Parker had wanted badly to become a career naval officer. His family was adamantly opposed. He bowed to their wishes but the restlessness never left him. "The period lying between the wars did not belong to John Parker," his cousin wrote in the "Groton School Quarterly" of 1942, following the report of Parker's death.

Indifferent to business success and undeterred by the passing years, Parker spent his energy on sports. With a gun, rod, glove, rein, tiller, or sheet it was for the fun he had, for the friends he made, and for distraction. His cousin said, "He needed more from life than the selling of securities and he took it" (Groton School Quarterly). During those two decades Parker joined the Norfolk Hunt Club to ride point-to-point races, and even in the more dangerous steeplechases. From the Union Boat Club he went single sculling on the Charles River. He cruised along the rocky, pine green coast of Maine. He sparred in Boston Amateur Athletics Association competitions and was already in his forties when a much younger contender knocked him out in the preliminaries for the national amateur bouts. None of these distractions brought him lasting satisfaction. He was among the earliest to pay attention when Hitler invaded Poland, plunging Europe into a war with Germany for the second time in a century.

All the men arrived in England with a valuable skill, either as qualified pilots or yachtsmen. The first of the twenty-two to take up "crown and anchor" was a crack aviator, William Erwin Gibson Taylor. The eldest son of U.S. Army colonel James G. Taylor, the boy spent his formative years as a dependent in a family that followed the father from one military assignment to the next. A grandfather had been a Union Army drummer boy in the Civil War. His godfather was Lieutenant (later, General of the Army) Douglas MacArthur. In the Philippines the Taylor family life was in a house built on stilts in the jungle, at the time of the Philippine Insurrection. An experience that stayed with the boy all his life was his discovery of the headless body of the man assigned to guard the family residence.

Taylor was accepted by the U.S. Naval Academy but an injury prevented him from entering. At age twenty-one he enrolled with the Guggenheim School of Aeronautical Engineering at New York University. There he got the lifelong desire to pilot aircraft. Before abandoning his technical studies Taylor enlisted as a private in the New York National Guard, at Miller Field, Long Island. The enlisting official put down "mechanic" as Taylor's vocation. At about the same time, the U.S. Navy was recruiting future pilots for its fledgling naval air force.

Taylor's application was accepted. He was commissioned and sent to Norfolk, Virginia, and flight school at Hampton Roads. Designated "Naval Aviator No. 4407" by the U.S. Navy's Bureau of Navigation, in the quaint language of the day he was authorized for duty "involving actual flying of aircraft, including dirigibles, balloons, and airplanes." Hopes of a career in naval aviation were dashed when he lost his active duty status after belt-tightening in the Navy Department resulted in personnel cuts. Taylor resigned his Navy commission when the chief of Marine Air offered him flying status, along with a commission as a second lieutenant in the U.S. Marine Corps Volunteer Reserve. In September 1929 Taylor became one of 146 aviators in the Aeronautic Organization of the Marine Corps. He had found a satisfactory place doing a job he loved in an atmosphere that suited his temperament and strengths. His fitness reports reflect a solid leader, capable, tactful, and industrious, and a "pleasing personality." Most essential, he was rated as "an exceptionally good pilot."

Throughout his service time in whatever branch or nation of the moment, Taylor regularly got an approving nod for his appearance in uniform, always impeccably cut and immaculate. With leading man looks, he made a dashing figure.

Bad luck (and congressional myopia) intervened once again in early summer 1933. Taylor was again made redundant due to "the necessity of effecting economies to keep within the reduced appropriations" (Maj. M. R. Thatcher communication, USMC, 11 September 1933, in William E. G. Taylor scrapbook, Garber Facility, National Air and Space Museum). Government jargon stays unchanged from one generation to the next and from one millennium to another. That same year, Hitler moved into Berlin's Reich Chancellery to become Germany's new leader, soon to be its dictator. Taylor found out that it was still not yet the right time for competent fliers in the U.S. military or elsewhere in the Allied nations. Only in Imperial Japan and Nazi Germany were military pilots highly valued, in demand, and fully employed. At an age when men generally are well along in their careers, Taylor was back at square one.

In the years that followed he flew as a copilot for United Airlines and in 1936 he bought a travel agency in New York City. On holiday in London in early autumn 1939 Taylor visited the U.S. naval attaché for air who was on the lookout for an American "observer" in the Royal Navy. The attaché encouraged Taylor to apply to the British admiral chairing a committee trying to find desperately needed pilots. Britain had declared war on Germany on September 3. Taylor's commission in the Royal Naval Volunteer Reserve came eleven days later.

London's *Evening Standard* ran a story headlined, "Recruit from the USA." The announcement is short and to the point: "At least one American has already joined our Forces. He is Captain William Taylor, formerly a military pilot in the United States Navy and in United Airlines. Captain Taylor . . . has been flying for fourteen years. He came to England a fortnight before the outbreak of war. And he has been enlisted now in the Fleet Air Arm. He will hold the rank of sub-lieutenant." At the age of thirty-four Taylor started anew. This time, his prospects were brighter.

The second American fighter pilot in the Fleet Air Arm was David Arnold van Epps, from Chicago. Flying aircraft was van Epps' passion, beginning with the Spartan School of Aeronautics in Tulsa, Oklahoma, and Randolph Field in San Antonio, Texas, where he earned his pilot wings. As Europe heated up van Epps wanted a piece of the action and headed north. The Canadian Air Service accepted him but Canada was not close enough to the fight so he changed direction and made his way to England.

Draper Kauffman graduated from the U.S. Naval Academy in 1933 but was denied a commission by the rules of the day due to his less-than-20/20 eyesight. He went to work as a young executive with the United States Lines Company, a steamship company. When Europe went to war he did not hesitate. By March 1940 Kauffman was in the French army as a driver with the American Volunteer Ambulance Corps. One of his fellow American brothers-in-arms, Lowell Bennett, wrote that Kauffman seemed to feel "the same way I do—I want to help anyone to help France—a country I came to love almost as much as my own" (USNI Oral History Program, May 1978 interview, #1, p. 56ff., Kauffman family archive).

This was an epochal time. Throughout May and early June the British Expeditionary Force was being driven to the sea. French resistance buckled. Kauffman was stationed at Neunkirch, roughly halfway between the two great surviving fortification anachronisms of the First World War, the Siegfried Line and the Maginot Line.

The first two weeks endured in his memory as "the most physically frightening experiences of my life and the most horror filled. Driving an ambulance through a great deal of shellfire, then picking up freshly wounded men in terrible pain." He recalled, "I learned to respect the infantryman, the ground puncher, deep, deep down from that moment on. Since then my respect for Marine and Army infantrymen has always been enormous, and I fully understand when I hear people talk about a soldier freezing and not being able to fire his rifle or running, I can't tell you how close I came to running several times" (ibid.)

Ambulances are not immune from becoming a battle target, Kauffman found out. He learned to cover the bright Red Cross emblem and American flag stenciled on the panels of his vehicle because they made an inviting bull's-eye. Many volunteers packed up and left under the unexpected pressure of this new juggernaut called Blitzkrieg. For his gallant performance, France awarded Kauffman the Croix de Guerre with Palm.

On June 22, 1940, as eighty-four-year-old Marshal Philippe Petain surrendered his country to Adolf Hitler, Kauffman was taken prisoner when attempting to ferry a group of wounded poilus (literally "hairy ones"—a World War I nickname for frontline French soldiers) through Wehrmacht lines. French army units near his hospital were cut off, and German artillery were zeroed in on the only road. Kauffman volunteered to take his ambulance to collect the wounded, going back repeatedly under heavy shellfire until the worst cases had all been moved to the hospital. Days later the hospital was overrun. Many injured soldiers had been evacuated, but there was no place for new wounded to go as the front retreated.

The local hospital was now in German hands. Kauffman loaded his ambulance with triage cases—men who would survive only if they got immediate surgery—and drove them through the German lines, ringing his bell and waving a white flag like a madman. The first time he bluffed his way in, delivered his cargo of wounded French soldiers to the German doctors, and went back for more. The second time the Germans accepted the wounded but seized the ambulance and "very respectfully and regretfully" took Kauffman captive.

Transported to the Luneville prisoner-of-war camp, he remained with fifteen other Americans from the ambulance corps, amid several thousand French troops.

Americans were a curiosity to the Germans who also wanted an opportunity to practice their English language skills. With a mix of mischief spiced with prescience, Kauffman taunted his captors by predicting that the war would soon all be over because the United States was not going to remain out of the conflict. He was fascinated by the absolute conviction of his young captors that their nation was the one most capable of governing the planet. The prison commandant questioned whether he had ever before visited Germany. On his arrival at the camp Kauffman stated that he had not been to Germany. Thinking it best to be consistent with his replies, he answered "No." The commander looked at the thick file of papers on his desk and continued, "I suppose you're not the Draper Kauffman who came to Germany as a midshipman in 1929 and went to Hamburg and Berlin" (ibid.). Turning the file pages he accurately described in detail other visits in 1936 and 1939. When Kauffman acknowledged that he had made the visits, the commander laughed. He was only teasing, he said, because he wanted to show his prisoner the omniscience of the Third Reich.

Kauffman said that American prisoners got "an honest-to-Goebbels education" (Joseph Goebbels was Hitler's minister of propaganda) in POW camp classrooms. The propaganda included graphic motion picture footage of the Luftwaffe sinking five British battleships. Not until he got to England did Kauffman learn that the whole thing was a fabrication, totally contrived and absolutely false in every respect.

Via a grapevine that included a wounded soldier, two French nurses, and an American Red Cross nurse, word eventually reached the U.S. Embassy in Paris that there was a group of Americans among the prisoners of war held in France. The U.S. naval attaché, Captain Roscoe Henry Hillenkoetter (later, vice admiral and the third director of the Central Intelligence Agency), got messages every few days from Kauffman's father (an admiral in Washington, D.C.) asking about his son. Hillenkoetter accepted Kauffman and the others when the Wehrmacht delivered them to the embassy. Each POW was on parole and made to sign a statement that stipulated they would not take up arms against Germany. As Kauffman's passport had been confiscated, the embassy issued a new one that was good for travel restricted specifically to France, Portugal, and Spain—en route to the United States. The passport was boldly endorsed, "Not Valid in the United Kingdom."

Kauffman had other ideas and did not feel bound by the parole. He left Paris and headed south through occupied France and Franco's Spain, then on to neutral Portugal where he was hired in Lisbon as a "second pantryman" aboard SS *Spiro*, bound for Scotland in the fullness of time. They steamed for forty-three nonstop days to a point near the mouth of the Amazon, then, up the U.S. coast as far as Boston where *Spiro* joined an escorted convoy across the Atlantic to the port of Methil, Scotland. Kauffman encountered some trouble getting ashore because of the restrictive stamp in his new American passport.

In an oral history, he told his interviewer at the Nimitz Library in Annapolis that "they let me go to London with instructions to report to the chief of police down there and to the American consul. I've always been fascinated by the fact that I went into the consular office and said, 'I have a mistake in my passport. Would you correct it for me? The passport says not valid for travel in England. Well, I'm already in England so obviously that's wrong.' The passport official answered, 'Why certainly,' and she stamped out [the restriction] and stamped a new one that said it was valid for travel in the United Kingdom for six months" (ibid).

Kauffman had never formally been demobilized, and traveled from Edinburgh to London on a free military travel pass, wearing his French army ambulance corps uniform. Soldiers mistook him for an officer and saluted smartly. This was the start of the year of British isolation when all of Europe fell to the German army. England's solitary resistance to Hitler's ambitions remained the one glimmer of light in a darkening world. In London Kauffman made a beeline to the Admiralty to ask about joining the Royal Navy. He got his commission as a sub-lieutenant Royal Naval Volunteer Reserve (Special Branch)—not a seagoing deck officer—on the same day. To his disappointment, the Royal Navy was no more prepared than Annapolis had been years before to let him serve as a deck officer. Instead, he became a bomb disposal officer and was taught how to defuse unexploded German ordnance. He did the job exceptionally well during the year of the Luftwaffe's most determined assault on Britain, and he did it very nearly without harm to himself.

At thirty-eight years of age, the pipe-smoking established Wall Street investment banker Alex Henry Cherry was an improbable candidate for freely choosing the perils of shot and shell over the comforts available in Manhattan. The only son of Latvian immigrants to the United States, Cherry was professionally successful and financially independent with the means to indulge expensive hobbies. His age put him well outside the scope of the draft. When his country started to mobilize for war, Cherry was in no danger whatever of being included in the national conscription net. He was safe. For Britain, he presented a valuable asset. Cherry was an experienced oceangoing yachtsman and licensed pilot, tickets that were eagerly sought by His Majesty's forces. The head test pilot for Lockheed, Milo Bircham, had taught him how to fly upside down. Cherry held licenses in navigation and wireless communication.

Cherry explained the impulse to enlist on the side of Britain as coming from the context of his generation: "Too young for World War I . . . we grew up with glowing accounts of the Lafayette Escadrille and the famous Americans who had flown its planes in combat . . . and [the] decorations bestowed upon them by the French nation was the pride of every American youth who hoped some day to emulate these great countrymen and achieve similar fame" (Alex Cherry, *Yankee RN*, London: Jarrolds, 1951). America's continuing neutrality and Neville Chamberlain's waffling appeasement of Hitler were profoundly dispiriting. For Cherry, the fall of France finally decided the question of where he would report. No other option existed. Britain now stood alone.

He was never shy about his extravagantly pro-British point of view. In his May 1940 letter to the Canadian minister of defense requesting a commission in the Royal Canadian Air Force, Cherry concluded with an unusual flourish for a son of the rebellious thirteen colonies, "Long live the King and Empire." More to the point he also wrote, "I cannot imagine a world as would exist should the Allies suffer defeat. With a bullying, brutally savage, ruthless, arrogant, Godless nation as would then dominate and influence the four corners of the world, I have arrived at the conclusion that life would not be worth living. That being the case, there is but one thing to do."

He especially idolized Royal Navy officers and when the toss of a coin determined his path to the Royal Navy, not the Royal Air Force, he could not have been more pleased. When the coin hit the floor it was Lincoln's head that turned up and Cherry "wanted to shake his hand." Heads meant the sea, his first love. With that, he left Struthers & Dean on Wall Street and joined the Royal Navy. Cherry described his experiences in *Yankee RN*.

In 1940 the German-American Bund Auxiliary, Inc., sued Edwin Fairman Russell for libel. They charged that Russell had published an article in the Russell family newspaper, *The Newark Ledger*, accusing the group of being involved with the National Socialist Party (the Nazi Party) in Germany. The complaint added that the article also wrongfully claimed the Bund operated training camps for Hitler sympathizers in the United States. The action was dismissed when the plaintiffs failed to appear in court.

Russell gave straightforward reasons for his decision to leave his country to join the British. It was a war of good against evil; there were no shades of gray. "I look back on my time in the RNVR with the greatest satisfaction and pride," he wrote in a letter to his relative by marriage, Prime Minister Winston Churchill, the day after the war ended. "Satisfied that events justified my enlisting in a 'foreign' service and proud to have been allowed to have served such a gallant people. Prior to the war I had spent a total of forty-eight hours in England . . . but I was so inspired by her fighting heart . . . that I slipped over the border to Canada and 'joined up.' My action was described as ill-advised, foolhardy, bravado and more. It may have been all of those at the time, but it turned out to be the most gratifying experience of my life." He wrote the letter aboard the cruiser USS *Oklahoma City* in the Pacific where he served after transferring to the U.S. Naval Reserve later in the war (Churchill Archives Center, 26 July 1945).

Russell arrived in England armed with a letter of introduction to the Duchess of Buccleuch, known as "Midnight Moll," who introduced him to her daughter. In turn, the daughter introduced him to Lady Sarah Spencer-Churchill who became his wife.

Sarah's maternal grandmother, Consuelo Vanderbilt, had restored the Duke of Marlborough's Blenheim Palace with her dowry. Backed by the Vanderbilt fortune her second husband, Jacques Balsan, helped to organize the all-American Lafayette Escadrille in World War I. In July 1939, on the eve of World War II, eighteen-year-old Sarah had a coming-out ball at Blenheim that is remembered as "the last great debut" in England. The Duke and Duchess of Kent, Winston Churchill, and Anthony Eden were among the nine hundred guests. It is said that the evening had the feel of the Duchess of Richmond's Grand Ball before Waterloo. Russell fit in with the Churchill tradition of encouraging foreigners to volunteer for England.

The great adventure in the Royal Navy started for Russell on October 21, 1941, on the transatlantic passage from Halifax to England aboard HMS *Ausonia*. His companion on the voyage was Bill Homans.

The most idealistic of the volunteers, at six feet four inches, William Perkins Homans was physically imposing, raw-boned, broad-shouldered, and extremely gifted. His grade school teacher at Brush Hill, in Milton, Massachusetts, said he was a genius boy. He came into her fifth grade class from schooling in France needing Yale University freshman–level reading materials and, to keep him challenged, advanced Latin. As an adult, the chain-smoking Homans with the "giant Apache face" (wrote a newspaper reporter) was also a moral force. What he saw on a visit to Nazi Germany had repulsed him. His son Peter wrote, "My father's reason for joining the RNVR before America entered the war was that he had done the 'traditional' European tour, I believe in the summer of 1939, and was horrified by what the Nazis were doing to the Jews when he was in Prague. He was born in 1923, so, I think he graduated from Harvard at 18 or perhaps earlier, possibly as young as 16, because I have the sense that he took that trip to Europe after he graduated from Harvard in 1938–1939" (Peter Homans correspondence with authors).

Bill Homans came from a prominent New England family with military traditions and considerable political influence in Massachusetts. Endicott Peabody, founder of Groton School for Boys, was a Homans ancestor who believed passionately that all born to privilege owed their country public service. Franklin Delano Roosevelt lauded Peabody. "As long as I live," wrote Roosevelt, "his influence will mean more to me than that of any other people next to my father and mother" (Otis L. Graham Jr. and Meghan Robinson, "Peabody Endicott," *Franklin D. Roosevelt, His Life and Times*, New York: Da Capo Press, 1985).

The Homans family championed freedom and duty to country. They believed there were things worth fighting and dying for. Homans' ancestors had fought on the side of the rebels against King George III during the American Revolution. Bill Homans' father served in the U.S. Cavalry in the early years of the twentieth century and his mother joined the Red Cross as a nurse in the U.S. Army in World War I. Blazing a trail for her nephew to follow, Aunt Helen Homans did duty as a volunteer nurse with the French army and was awarded the Croix de Guerre in 1916 as she lay fatally ill with pneumonia in France.

Homans knew the importance of the battle that Britain waged and he rushed to play an active part. He wanted to fly the British Spitfire fighter and applied to the Royal Air Force in Canada. His immense size defeated the aircraft's tight cockpit. With a lot of experience handling small sailboats, he opted to join the Royal Navy instead. His decision to fight for Britain and King George VI was greeted with approval by parents as well as friends. Later the scope of his humanity included saving the life of an enemy combatant who ditched in the Irish Sea. Though it nearly impoverished him, Homans went on to defend human rights all of his life.

Another volunteer in his late thirties was Oswald Birrell Deiter from Dansville, New York. Deiter was a skilled osteopath and obstetrician who had worked his way through the Philadelphia School of Osteopathy. In 1927 he was awarded a fellowship for advanced study in medicine in London, where he specialized in obstetrics at Queen Charlotte's Hospital (a famous West London maternity hospital—the oldest in the country) and several city clinics. In 1933, while a young assistant osteopath at the Hertfordshire Health Home, he burst into media headlines when an aged female patient whom he had treated kindly left him £20,000 ($100,000), a very large fortune at that time, in her will. Deiter got the bequest but not before a fierce court challenge by the woman's relatives. He then studied in Korea, Japan, and China and pioneered osteopathy in Germany in 1936. His sterling medical reputation won him the prestigious job of resident physician at Champneys, the famous English health spa at Tring. With his English wife, Ellaline Macey, Deiter set up house in London's exclusive Park Lane district where they led a comfortable life. At the beginning of the war Deiter continued with his medical practice, despite the bombing, and doing his military "bit" as an occasional soldier in the Home Guard.

The Home Guard was a branch of the British Army made up of part-time, mostly over-the-hill volunteers. The men were either too old for active service or employed in occupations that could not afford to lose them, or both. Entry was supposedly restricted to British-born men with British parents. However in July 1940, after the fall of France, Charles Sweeney, a U.S. soldier of fortune, helped to raise an all-American Home Guard contingent manned by U.S.-born residents of London.

Sweeney was a tireless socialite and consummate name-dropper who lived his life meeting and exploiting people with name recognition and power. The result this time was the one-hundred-man 1st American Motorised Squadron. Sweeney wired his father in New York, "Can you obtain any submachine guns." The reply came, "One hundred Tommy guns with 100,000 rounds of ammunition en route to you donated by the Thompson Company" (Charles Sweeney, *Sweeney*, Canterbury: Harrop Press, 1990). The ordinary Home Guard was not as blessed with modern weaponry; they sometimes did their drill with sticks in lieu of the scarce rifles that were needed for actual frontline troops. The American unit also contributed their private automobiles and had them repainted at their own expense in olive drab. Oswald Deiter was among the first to join. The squadron was based close to Grosvenor Square, near the U.S. Embassy. Their left uniform sleeve bore the addition of a red American eagle badge.

In January 1941 on Horse Guards Parade, Prime Minister Churchill personally came to inspect them. It was a proud day for Deiter and his fellow Americans. They formed three troops under the command of Brigadier General Wade Hampton Hayes, a Virginian by birth who had fought in the Spanish-American War and was on General Pershing's staff in the First World War. Hayes appeared on newsreels to explain, "We started the American Unit because our homes are here, and we wanted to show in some practical way that we were ready, with the British, to share the responsibility of defending their soil. We would have felt ashamed of ourselves if we had sat on the sidelines and done nothing." He added, "We believe we have a stake in this country hardly less than the British people themselves." Hayes also said that he and his men had received many cables and letters from the United States indicating that Americans at home were fully supportive, "short of war" ("Prime Minister Inspects London American Guard," Universal Newsreel, 1940, YouTube).

In March 1941 both the *Times* and the *Daily Telegraph* announced that "O. B. Deiter, Osteopath, entered the RNVR." There is a photograph of Deiter in the *Illustrated London News* above the caption "A well-known American osteopath, practicing in the West End of London, who has joined the Royal Navy" (31 May 1941). Deiter was commissioned a sub-lieutenant and trained at the Lansing College. The news item and photograph appeared in papers throughout the United States, in towns where Deiter once lived. The press arm of the British government lost no time in letting the American cousins know that one of their own had made a commitment that other Americans could follow. Deiter had quickly shelved his medical profession to become a line officer—a ship driver—in the Royal Navy.

By coincidence, Surgeon Lieutenant Francis Mason Hayes was commissioned on the day HMS *Broadwater* was lost, October 18, 1941. He was the first-born and only son of parents who idolized him. They lived in Pelham Manor, New York. A niece remembered Francis for being "what we girls used to call 'a dish.' He was tall, lean and handsome with a ready smile and a love of girls, jokes and tennis" (Ann Davenport Dixon letter, 20 October 2003). He also played football and polo, sang in a Glee Club (a musical group of male voices), and acted. Hayes transferred to Cambridge University to complete his medical studies, motivated to switch schools by falling for a girl nicknamed Tigger. The impact must have been startling love at first sight because Hayes left it up to his sister to explain to Yale University, and his parents, why he had decamped so suddenly for London. He got his training literally in the fires of the Blitz, doing emergency surgery on wounded survivors. Hayes died when his ship sank with all hands west of Ireland, a torpedo casualty in the Battle of the Atlantic. His wife, Georgette (the same Tigger), and a four-year-old son, John Peter, survived him.

John "Jack" Edward Hampson ranched a handsome property with his father in Bardsdale, California, on the edge of Los Padres National Forest. Flying got the best of the son's attention and by the age of twenty-three he had a job as a civilian transport pilot. Hampson took a physical at the U.S. Naval Station, San Diego, with the aim of becoming a Marine Corps Reserve aviator, but vision problems—he needed glasses—ended hopes of a military career in aviation. His application was rejected.

New York businessman Edward Mortimer Ferris was the first "sea officer" to report to the Royal Naval College. Ferris also had an extensive blue-water sailing background. His father had often entered his yawl, *Malay*, in the Bermuda races and Ed and his younger brothers, Henry and Ray, were the crew. Nothing could slow Ed's determination to head for Canada and "to stick around until I was either accepted or turned down," he said. He added, "Anyway, they got tired of saying No" (29 June 1941 correspondence forwarded to Vice Admiral W. J. Whitworth, KCB, DSO, Charlotte Hammond collection). Ed Ferris was friends with Charles Burnham Porter, the third Royal Navy College arrival, and another sailing enthusiast. Porter's father was a physician and his mother, Margaret Cockran Dewar, kept house. Harvard followed St. Mark's School but study was not Porter's strong suit and his undergraduate academic achievement wavered between inconspicuous and disaster.

At the end of his second sophomore year he dropped out of college altogether following a "mild discussion with the Dean" about grades (conversation with Allen Bigelow, Porter's nephew). Porter drifted from one job to another until 1932 when he entered the business of real estate. In 1938 he cruised with Samuel Eliot Morison to the West Indies where Morison gathered information for what became a Pulitzer Prize–winning biography of Christopher Columbus. The years of the Great Depression in the United States were lean but a successful career enabled Porter (he was called Burnham by friends and family) to indulge his passion for canvas, wind, and the sea. He built a thirty-two-foot auxiliary cutter, *Roarin' Bessie*, that he sailed extensively in waters from New England to the tropics. Like others among the volunteers, poor eyesight spoiled his application for the U.S. Navy.

A brutally sharp end to a brand-new marriage got Peter Greene Morison to review his priorities. He grew up a neighbor of Bill Homans and also came from an accomplished New England family. In his early twenties Peter Morison married a young woman against the wishes of her wealthy family. The couple settled in Maine where Morison went to work at Bath Iron Works, building warships. The small-town atmosphere, her husband's apparent lowly status, and the continued disapproval of her parents unnerved the bride. About a year after the wedding Morison came home to a good-bye letter left in an empty house; his young wife had bolted for her old home. Morison's father, Samuel Eliot Morison, was promoted to rear admiral and put in charge of writing the U.S. Navy's fifteen-volume history of World War II. In 1979 the U.S. Navy named one of its fast frigates in his honor. Much was expected of Morison males.

John Matthew Leggat was a rosy-cheeked twenty-two-year-old from Los Angeles, California. No record has been uncovered to explain his motivation to travel six thousand miles to a country notorious for its perpetual wet cloud cover, its back put up against a wall by a Nazi juggernaut, and go to war in the Royal Navy. But he showed himself to be a born naval officer who rose to be an intrepid commanding officer.

An austere and uncompromising father, Colonel Henry Ashley Ripley (all the Ripleys bore the name Henry) offered his son the Army via West Point or the Navy by way of Annapolis. Henry Fremont Ripley was born at Camp Keithley on Lake Lanao in Mindanao where his father commanded the Philippine Scouts. Left to his own decisions young Ripley wanted to be an artist. Instead, George M. Young of the Second District, North Dakota, appointed him to the Naval Academy. Ripley stood 390th in the class of 1926 and had the nickname Rip.

"He can sing," records the U.S. Naval Academy's yearbook, *Lucky Bag*, thumbnail biography. "He used to set his alarm clock every morning for half an hour before reveille so he could get up and practice scales. A pair of shoes broke him of the habit in a month." Signs of awkwardness around women showed up early. In the midshipman argot of the day, "He was a hopeless Red Mike as far as dragging goes but he generally managed to be on hand for the hops" (*Lucky Bag*, Annapolis: U.S. Naval Academy, 1926). Fifteen years later, in 1941 when his marriage failed, Ripley scuttled his naval career, dismantled the foundations of a well-ordered life, resigned his regular commission as a lieutenant in a peacetime U.S. Navy, and volunteered to go to war as a junior officer in the Royal Navy. Ripley left behind a one-year-old son who he would see again only three more times in his life.

Broken marriages were common among the U.S. citizens in the Royal Navy: Fourteen of the volunteers divorced at least once. Two—Taylor and Porter—never married. Seven of them married English women: Ferris, Morison, Deiter, Stilwell, Hoague, Hayes, and Russell.

In the late 1930s John Albert Stilwell joined his father on a trip to England to help establish a theater program and advertising business called Stilwell, Derby & Co, in Blackburn, Lancashire. He met his future wife, Marjorie Taylor, there.

David Gibson had the tickets the British looked for in its U.S. applicants. The Royal Navy wanted a mirror image, with an American twang, of the comparable social class expected in their homegrown officers. Some of the men in the Eagle Squadron hint that the Royal Air Force weighed pilot abilities more heavily than breeding and education. The Royal Navy made no such concessions. Gibson's preparatory school, like Peter Morison's, was St. Paul's and he followed his brother into Yale University, but did not graduate as planned with the class of 1942. Gibson said, "At the end of my junior year at Yale in May 1941 I went to Halifax to see Admiral Bonham Carter . . . the upshot of my visit to the Admiral was to volunteer to join the RNVR." Bonham-Carter was a good friend of Gibson's British-born mother; she had a summer property in

Nova Scotia where Bonham-Carter had been a visitor over many happy weekends. When the twenty-one-year-old American showed up, Bonham-Carter commissioned him on the spot.

Gurdan Buck was in his mid-thirties and several years into farming his land in Maryland when Hitler went to war. Buck and his wife, Elizabeth, had their first child, a daughter, at the farm. He knew England well from his undergraduate days at Cambridge University. By education, vocation, and interests Buck too came from comfortable financial roots. He also had extensive ocean sailing experience having cruised along the U.S. Atlantic Coast, the English Channel, and the Mediterranean.

George Hoague went to Noble and Greenough (founded in 1866 and informally known as "Nobles") and received his AB at Harvard in 1926. He trained as a naval architect and remained a lifelong avid yachtsman. He also taught German and mathematics at Belmont Hill, a private school, but his passion was sailing and the sea. The greater part of his spare time was spent cruising in small boats. He navigated, crewed, or skippered yachts three times to Bermuda, numerous times to Nova Scotia and Newfoundland, and twice across the North Atlantic. He was precisely the sort of man the Royal Navy was looking for.

Gentleman farmer and scion of an old Virginia family, Edmund Webster Kittredge came fully prepared for the Royal Navy through his undergraduate naval training in the Reserve Officers' Training Corps (ROTC). Kittredge's father was William Gholson Kittredge, a Virginia gentleman farmer and lawyer. Edmund was educated at Hackley School, New York, 1925–29, and Yale University 1929–33. He spent his undergraduate years idling along with modest academic achievement, free to spend a weekly allowance of $100 at the time of the Great Depression, when the average weekly manufacturing job paid $16.89 and a physician got $61. He graduated from Yale's Sheffield School of Engineering in 1933 and worked in finance in Cincinnati in the years between 1933 and 1941. Kittredge was an accomplished yachtsman who sailed with his father in a knockabout sloop. In 1937 he cruised with Bill Anderson who later bought the firm of John G. Alden where another U.S. volunteer in the Royal Navy, George Hoague, had worked as a naval architect.

After Yale, Kittredge had moved to Cincinnati and a career in banking and finance, calling it "f'nance." He loved the First World War and its heroes and despised Roosevelt, communists, and socialism. He most valued "loyalty, honor, and courage" he said. "Diligence, honesty, and thrift" were dull and bourgeois. But neither a good life nor banking could distract his attention from the new war in Europe. Kittredge was given permission by his local draft board to leave the United States for England for no longer than six months. As acceptable camouflage he declared that his intention was to volunteer for British "civilian defense work." There is no record of why the draft board agreed to this odd, inappropriate explanation as a substitute for service in the armed forces of the United States.

Konow was an American by choice. Carl Frederik Sophus Vilhelm Konow was born to Caroline Amalie, the Baroness Juel-Brockdorff. A grandfather five times removed was Niels Juel, the seventeenth-century naval hero of the Battle of Køge Bugt in the Scanian War. Juel's reward was the estate and castle of Valdemars Slot where Konow spent his childhood.

Konow was born to the sea. At fifteen he became a volunteer apprentice and then a cadet in the Royal Danish Navy. Two years later he left for Asia with the East Asiatic Company, an able seaman on *Selandia*, the world's first ocean-going diesel motor ship. In 1922 and again the following year, he sailed on the school ship *København*, a five-mast, steel-hulled bark. (*København* went on to meet her fate not long afterward. She departed the River Plate on passage from Montevideo to Melbourne and vanished, "without leaving as much as an identifiable splinter behind her, or the bones of one of her forty-five boys." Her last radio message was "All's well" [Lincoln Paine, *Ships of the World*, New York: Houghton Mifflin Harcourt, 1997]).

At Greenwich, his fellow officers-in-training called him by his lifelong nickname, Leaping Dane, so called because of his unusual nimbleness on deck when racing in 6-meter yachts. To close friends and family he was "Leaping." Konow cleared U.S. immigration speaking English, French, and German in addition to his native Danish. He came looking for adventure and a new life.

Konow did his pilot training at Brooks Field, San Antonio, Texas, and for a few years flew the U.S. mail. Other airmen who got their wings at Brooks Field during that time were Nathan Farragut Twining, Charles Lindbergh, and Curtis LeMay. Konow regularly interrupted his American life to return to Denmark to take part in yacht races, always coming home by ocean liner as a passenger in first class. When war came he was in New York working as a yacht broker for Sparkman and Stephens. The German occupation of Denmark in April 1940 galvanized him. Konow badly wanted to pilot military aircraft but at forty-one years of age he was too old by far.

Derek Armitage Lee's family owned the world-famous specialty textile mill of Arthur H. Lee & Sons. Lee was a graduate of Dartmouth College, class of 1934, where he took up fencing and boxing, and he was already in England in 1939 when war came. He immediately enlisted in the Royal Navy as a rating and later commissioned into the RNVR.

The twenty-two men formed a part of the vanguard of U.S. citizens who wanted to defend Britain. Other Americans volunteered for the British army and air force. They reacted much in the same manner as their forebears, twenty-five years earlier. World War I Americans had rushed to join the British and French in their war against the Kaiser, even as the United States remained neutral in the years between 1914 and 1917. In the early stages of World War II Americans made the transition to British forces of every uniform pattern and hue. Damn the legalities. Any cultural differences took a backseat to the common purpose. "We Yanks came for various reasons," said a pilot. He explained, "We were supported by an enthusiastic attitude about crushing the Axis and a great deal of compassion for the folks in the United Kingdom." American volunteer fighter pilots in the Eagle Squadron invited the popular U.S. ambassador John Gilbert Winant (like Gibson and Morison, a graduate of St. Paul's) to be their guest of honor on the first Thanksgiving that Winant spent in England. Winant was tall, mildly stooped, and with a prominent chin and dark hair. He reminded people of Abraham Lincoln.

Not everyone wore navy or air force blue. Some put on British army khaki. "Americans Join the Army," proclaimed the *Times* when the first group of university graduates arrived to take up commissions in the King's Royal Rifle Corps, an infantry regiment. Winant made personal contact with them and wrote in his memoirs, *A Letter from Grosvenor Square*, that the United States "has every reason to be proud" of these American volunteers (Hodder & Stoughton, 1947). The first band of young men to join the British army in England stayed at his apartment when they came to town.

Heyward Cutting was one of them. The others were Charles G. Bolte, Jack Brister, David Cox, and Bill Durkee. It was to be a last, brief luxury before they departed with their regiment. Cutting joined the 60th Regiment of Foot, the famous Green Jackets which in colonial days during the French and Indian Wars bore the name Royal Americans. A Dartmouth College graduate and Rhodes scholar at Oxford, Bolte lost a leg at the hip in the battle of El Alamein. Cox lost his life in the fighting around El Alamein, and Brister was killed in action just before the surrender in North Africa. Durkee was shot through both knees in a Messerschmitt 109 aircraft strafing, and Cutting was twice wounded but went on to fight the Wehrmacht through Italy and Austria and was cited for gallantry. He ended the war in the rank of major. Winant called the men his "Five Musketeers." He wrote, "It takes great courage to join a foreign fighting force in another country, even though you believe in the cause for which that country is fighting" (*A Letter from Grosvenor Square*).

Their action calls to mind a passage, from Bryant Perrett's book titled *Impossible Victories,* on the taking of the Taku Forts in China in 1859: Lying at anchor outside the bar was the flagship of the U.S. Navy's Asiatic Squadron, commanded by Commodore Josiah Tattnall. As a midshipman Tattnall had fought against the British during the War of 1812, but for him that lay in the past and he was not enjoying the spectacle of two British gunboats being knocked apart. He had his steam launch called away and, disregarding the Chinese fire, traveled upstream until he was alongside HMS *Plover.* Clambering aboard, he suggested to Admiral Hope that the launch be used to evacuate the wounded. Hope had already accepted gratefully when Tattnall observed that his boat's crew had become involved in the fighting.

"What have you been doing, you rascals?" he shouted as they returned, powder-stained, to their own craft. "Don't you know we're neutrals?"

"Beg pardon, sir," came the reply, "They were a bit short-handed on the bow gun and we thought it no harm to give them a hand while we were waiting."

Tattnall could only grin at Hope before remarking, "I guess blood must be thicker than water!" It was a remark that would go down in the history of both navies (Bryant Perrett, *Impossible Victories*, London: Cassell Military Paperbacks, 2000).

Altruism was not the only motive for volunteers in those years. In January 1941, a forty-seven-year-old medically retired U.S. Army captain, partially deaf and suffering from chronic bronchitis, recruited 100 American fighter pilots and 250 ground crew for Chiang Kai-shek's miniscule Republic of China Air

Force. Claire Lee Chennault, a distant relative of Confederate general Robert E. Lee, needed men between the ages of twenty-three and twenty-eight who were prepared to resign their U.S. military commissions to join the American Volunteer Group (AVG).

The pay was double what they made in the U.S. Army, plus a $500 bonus for each Japanese aircraft shot down. Disguised as engineers, Chennault's mercenaries went to China and Burma where they painted the nose of their P-40 fighter aircraft with the toothy tiger shark emblem. Thus was born one of the most distinctive insignia of World War II. In the seven months of their existence, before they were recommissioned as U.S. Army Air Corps officers, the Flying Tigers shot down 299 Japanese aircraft with another 153 "probable kills." On rare ceremonial occasions they wore their Chinese uniforms, otherwise they flaunted their independence with loud shirts, cowboy boots, and hard drinking. British officers were scandalized by their brashness in colonial Rangoon. Japanese radio described them as "unprincipled bandits" (James Kerr, "Warbird the Men and the Planes . . . ," *Sun Sentinel*, 6 June 1988). The American Volunteer Group in China was the first U.S. force to see action against the Japanese.

3 Come to England, Passport Not Required

The Royal Navy volunteers got a movie semblance of their experience in a 1958 Carol Reed romance drama called *The Key*, starring William Holden as ocean tug skipper Lieutenant Commander David Ross, RNR, an American. The film is set in 1941 when poorly armed tugs were sent to "U-boat alley" (fictional, but it might have been any place offshore the British Isles) to rescue crippled Allied merchant ships. Trevor Howard plays Chris Ford, Ross' British foil. Sophia Loren is refugee Stella. The key to her apartment has passed from one lover to another—all tugboat captains and all dead. The key is a harbinger of death and Ross is number four. A good deal is made of Ross' nationality and of his frustrations with the chronic shortage of available material and spare parts support at this early phase of the war in Britain. In one scene, a disappointed and frustrated Ross has his request for better guns and armor plating denied again, but he is offered a sop with the news that the Japanese have attacked the U.S. Pacific Fleet at Pearl Harbor.

The United States is now in the war, he is told. Preoccupied with his own unmet requirements Ross responds dryly, "On which side?" The story is based on Jan de Hartog's 1941 book, *Stella*. Most of the seagoing tugs left Holland for England when the Germans invaded. De Hartog's tale is about the lives of the Dutch tugboat captains and the enigmatic woman in her flat.

In all respects the British, both the military and the civilian side, accept Ross without question while commenting good-naturedly on his accent and American style of doing business. In 1952, coasting on the phenomenal success of Hugh Hastings' London production of the comedy *Seagulls over Sorrento*,

Hollywood toyed with the idea of making an adventure drama out of the play, re-titled *Crest of the Wave*. Hedda Hopper wrote that Van Johnson was to be cast as an American who joins the Royal Navy. Nothing came of it and the detail is included here only to show that there was a certain resonance—cultural opposites?—of a British naval uniform on an American citizen. Alex Cherry's book, *Yankee RN*, published to considerable acclaim in 1951, could very likely have given Hollywood the idea.

The subtext of *The Key* was the seamless transition from one culture into another by a man who chose to help a battered people, who shared the little there was, and who was "mucking in" with them to do a dirty job. The movie was a hit overseas. The film's theme plays on how traditional British reserve meets laconic American pragmatism, spiced with irreverence. The result has comic as well as dramatic appeal. The message is that contrasting backgrounds can get the job done when men are united by a great cause. The British were surprised and grateful for the American volunteers among them.

For their part, the real volunteers had no problem locking arms with their English cousins. Making the fictional David Ross a commanding officer fits the character and capabilities of his real-life contemporaries. Taylor and van Epps commanded fighter squadrons; Deiter commanded the gunboat HMML *115;* Ferris was captain of a destroyer escort, HMS *Byard*; Konow captained HM *LST 198;* Gibson commanded three ships, including the Flower-class corvette HMS *Willowherb* and the Captain-class destroyer escort HMS *Gardiner*, on their return to the United States; Cherry probably commanded HMS *Braithwaite* between U.S. ports. Leggat skippered USS *LCS (L) 44* when the Americans discovered how well the Royal Navy had trained him to command. Derek Lee was appointed first lieutenant of HMS *Bickerton* and later became the gallant commanding officer of a unit of Anglo-American commandos operating against Japanese forces in the Far East. Kauffman went on to become an admiral in the U.S. Navy and led thousands of officers, ratings, and midshipmen.

Eleven of twenty-two selected for command responsibility is a high percentage, even accounting for the supercharged contingencies of a world war.

Americans could not willy-nilly put on a British uniform. There were considerable hurdles to overcome regarding procedure, including Anglo-U.S. political sensibilities, the oath of allegiance, questions of citizenship, obligations of service, and much besides. An enabling framework needed to be built. In late summer 1939, when war with Germany had become inevitable, discussions within the Admiralty and elsewhere in Whitehall focused on the possibility of enlisting American subjects as officers in the Royal Navy. The Admiralty's director of appointments was informed privately by both the U.S. naval attaché, Captain Alan Goodrich Kirk, and the naval air attaché that former Navy pilots who had been relegated to Reserve duty following personnel cutbacks in the 1930s—Royal Navy volunteer William Erwin Gibson Taylor's case exactly—might be a fruitful source of eager recruits for the Fleet Air Arm in the event of war.

With the Neutrality Act, U.S. law had probably gone further than international law in forbidding its citizens to enter the armed forces of belligerent nations. A loophole seemed to be that international law did not prevent a warring nation such as Great Britain from enlisting volunteers who were American citizens as long as there was no organized recruiting within the United States. Of course, it was necessary that an officer should resign his U.S. commission before offering his services to Britain so as not to provoke U.S. authorities, to say nothing of stirring up the "America First" lobby who demonstrated loudly and often against any involvement in another European war.

It was the opinion of the U.S. naval attaché that the tendering of resignations would not be obstructed by the U.S. Navy because of the valuable experience the pilots would gain. Britain's Foreign Office, informally consulted, raised no objections to the proposals.

There was another issue to resolve. It was expected that some Americans would be deterred by the oath of allegiance. An oath to the King could lead directly to loss of citizenship. As far as London was concerned, under the Defence Regulations of 1939, an alien could be enlisted in any of His Majesty's forces as if he were a British subject, and there was no limit to the number of aliens who were able to serve together at any one time in any corps or unit. To encourage Americans, Britain needed to find means of dodging the requirement for an oath and thus avoid the implied renunciation of U.S. citizenship.

There was no standard procedure.

Those who voluntarily entered the Royal Air Force had to take the oath of allegiance contained in the attestation paper in accordance with the Air Force Act, but the oath was not required by those called up for conscripted service under the National Service Act of 1939. In other words, there was no governmental requirement that in order to serve as an airman a man must take the oath of allegiance. As for the Royal Navy, ratings—enlisted personnel—were not required to attest or take an oath at all but merely had to sign an engagement to serve honestly and faithfully for a specified period. Those who entered directly as officers were not required to take the oath of allegiance, nor did they have to sign an engagement commitment. The general practice was for them to complete an application form stating only that they understood the conditions of service. On the other hand, although the Royal Marines were part of the Royal Navy, recruits were required to take an oath of allegiance, as they were for the Army. Consistency in these matters was not a hallmark of the British military establishment. U.S. authorities were similarly contradictory, most especially after the Japanese attacked Pearl Harbor and Germany declared war on the United States. By summer 1942, the HM Dockyard commodore in Bermuda (HMS *Malabar*) could blithely write to the local U.S. consul general, "Sir, I have the honour to inform you that Lieutenant A. H. Cherry, RNVR, an American citizen, is travelling on leave to the United States [and] I should be grateful if the United States Immigration authorities could be informed that time did not permit of his obtaining a visa for entry" (Alex Cherry note, Michael Sabatell collection).

When Charles Sweeney suggested the creation of an American military unit in the British army, he proceeded very cautiously indeed. Ever sensitive to the Neutrality Act as well as citizenship considerations, he offered the vague idea of American volunteers "attached to the London Area HQ" of the Home Guard with "similar" ranks to the British army. Nothing was said about an oath of allegiance. This was thin camouflage but it worked. The result was the 1st American Motorised Squadron. The U.S. military attaché in London at that time, General Lee, could have stopped any such scheme in its tracks. He apparently did nothing to interfere and his autobiography, *The Journal of General Raymond E. Lee 1940–41,* is silent on the subject of Americans in British military service (James Leutze, editor, Boston: Little, Brown, 1971).

Sir Archibald Sinclair, secretary of state for Air, wrote to Sir Alexander Hardinge, King George VI's private secretary. He outlined the difficulties that the oath of allegiance was causing and advised that discussions had taken place between the Admiralty, the War Office, and the Air Ministry and reported that there had been no objections with regard to waiving the oath. Further, Sinclair hoped "very much that in these exceptional circumstances His Majesty would be willing to approve of a special regulation which would dispense altogether with the necessity for the taking of the oath" (National Archives File ADM 1/11259, British Records Office). Sinclair indicated that he had already arranged the drafting of such a regulation for its consideration by the Home Policy Committee.

On June 18, 1940, following agreement by the War Cabinet Home Policy Committee, King George VI approved the proposal. The Ministry of Information further blunted the issue with a decision to offer British citizenship to any American who lost his U.S. citizenship. By then, Taylor was already on active service. None of the RNVR volunteers let citizenship issues become an obstacle. Derek Lee told his brother Rigby that if the British should question his loyalty to the King, he would assure them that he was just as loyal as the prime minister's mother who was also an American. Lady Randolph Churchill, the former Jenny Jerome, had been born in the New York borough of Brooklyn.

On the official side, various parts of the government clearly did not communicate—never mind coordinate—policy or procedures.

The oath decision was important. An article in the *New York Herald Tribune* on July 3, 1941, concerned the refusal by U.S. immigration authorities to readmit an American citizen, Philip Stegerer, because he had fought in the Royal Canadian Air Force. He had joined the RCAF when it was still necessary to take the oath of allegiance to the King. Word spread quickly and far. With a dateline of July 4, 1940, the *Canberra Times* (Australia) published the story. "The United States Board of Inquiry has ruled that Philip Stegerer, aged 26, of Washington, has forfeited his United States citizenship by joining the Canadian active services, from which he was honorably discharged as medically unfit. The Board refused permission for Stegerer to return to the United States. It is believed that the case is a precedent as a result of which hundreds may be deprived of citizenship because of allegiance to His Majesty." Stegerer told the media, "We have been residents of the US since before the Revolutionary War. I come to Canada to fight for democracy and I wind up a guy without a country, without a job and without a dime. Oh, gosh!" Stegerer's subsequent fate is unknown.

The British Foreign Office worried that the treatment meted out to Stegerer would affect the recruitment of American volunteers elsewhere. In the end, whatever branch of British service U.S. citizens joined, or whatever oath or affirmation might have been made, there was minimal to no penalty or censure when they came home again. David Gibson described how he had come back to the United States to be a "100% American once more [but] that I had unknowingly lost my American citizenship by serving in the Armed Force of a foreign government. To regain it I simply had to recite the Pledge of Allegiance before a U.S. Consular Officer!" (correspondence, Eric Gibson collection).

The nationality saga clearly shows that there was no consistent policy impartially applied, especially among immigration officials in the United States. Stegerer's treatment illustrates the U.S. government's confused reaction to concerns about national security. A decision to deny citizenship could be as simple as the whim of the immigration officer or board of inquiry hurriedly assembled to monitor resident aliens. An Anglo-American Fleet Air Arm pilot, David Foster related the following:

> I was born in London on May 24, 1920, to parents who were both native-born Americans. I held two nationalities, British and American. Understandably, in 1939 at Cambridge University I volunteered to join the Fleet Air Arm of the Royal Navy. I was called for duty on April 1, 1940, at Royal Navy Barracks Gosport. I had an exciting war serving in the Middle East, Europe, Far East and the Pacific and ended up a Lieutenant Commander, DSO, DSC and bar and commanding officer of the TBF (Grumman torpedo bomber) squadron on HMS *Victorious*. I lost my U.S. nationality on joining the RNVR. I was approached to join the Eagle Squadron but preferred to stay in the Royal Navy. After the war I applied for a U.S. visa on my British passport to take a job with Colgate. The U.S. Embassy in London would not do this as they claimed I had the right to U.S. nationality and issued me with a U.S. passport.

David Foster became chairman and CEO of Colgate.

A further incentive for American volunteers was offered in August 1940, when the Admiralty confirmed that if the United States became involved in hostilities, U.S. citizens serving in any branch of the Royal Navy could be released to join American forces if that was their wish. Most of the volunteers took the opportunity when the time came. Besides a change in uniform style, the difference in pay was huge. The monthly $67.50 for a two-striper in the Royal Navy in 1943 rocketed to $520 in the U.S. Navy. When Derek Lee first joined the Royal Navy as a rating, his daily pay was two shillings and sixpence, plus an allowance of three pence for clothing and another three pence for rum. (There were twenty shillings in the old pound and twelve pence in each shilling. A pound was worth about $5 at that time.) The immense financial inequity was noted by many of the volunteers who transferred to U.S. service from British military service, especially pilots. In the letter notifying him of his appointment in the rank of "Temporary Lieutenant, RNVR," Alex Cherry was informed that his monthly pay would be £20.5 shillings. Cherry thought that the gap was the chief motivation for making the change. In his opinion the men "requested for transfer in view of [the] differential of pay between the two navies" (correspondence, Michael Sabatell collection).

For British officials, documentary caution to protect its U.S. volunteers prevailed to the end. For instance, Edmund Kittredge's official discharge papers from the Royal Navy in June 1946 specifically noted "Personnel do not take an Oath of Allegiance on entry or during service with the Royal Navy." Ever protective of their American volunteers, the Admiralty further sought to shield them from legal hassles with a clear disclaimer that their service had not violated U.S. law.

At first, it was felt that the best for both sides was to give as little prominence to the issue as possible as it was thought that this would help to deflect political repercussions. The resolution did not last long. The publicity value of Americans in British service was just too hot and irresistible.

An officer selection board convened to interview persons with flying experience who might be suitable for temporary Royal Naval Volunteer Reserve (Air) commissions; the Air indicated service with the Fleet Air Arm. William Taylor was the first to be brought aboard. The RNVR was popularly known as the "Wavy Navy" because its sleeve rank rings undulated while those of a regular officer were straight. The "wavy" rank lace was a prewar distinction that became more obvious when thousands of wartime officers started to appear. There was also a distinction between the Royal Naval Reserve (ex–Royal Navy officers or experienced Merchant Navy deck officers, who had another variation of rank lace) and the RNVR who were gifted amateurs beloved of legend. There was a saying in the wartime Navy: "The RNR are officers trying to be gentlemen; the RNVR are gentlemen trying to be officers, and the RN are neither, trying to be both."

For the United Kingdom in her desperate early days, recruitment of pilots from the United States for the Royal Navy's Fleet Air Arm was a priority. Among the main difficulties envisaged was the Admiralty's need to consider how best the bona fides and character of each volunteer would be established. U.S. representatives, including Captain Kirk, the naval attaché, could not be publicly involved in a vetting procedure. The attaché advised that it was possible for officers in U.S. armed forces to get copies of their official annual officer evaluations (reports of fitness, the U.S. Navy calls them). The documents might then be discreetly passed to the Admiralty via a third party, probably a private individual. A suitable candidate would be informed through the third party when to come to England.

Herein lay another difficulty. A passport could not be issued in the United States without the applicant stating he would not join the armed forces of a foreign nation. To navigate around this obstacle it was necessary for a volunteer to first make his way to Canada where a travel document was not at that time required of U.S. citizens. The question then arose how the men would get to England without a passport, as ordinarily shipping companies would not accept undocumented passengers. The Admiralty consulted the Immigration Branch who advised that an arrangement with either Canadian Pacific or the Cunard White Star Line could allow volunteers to embark without a passport. No difficulties were envisaged in making such an adjustment and it was further agreed that volunteers would have the cost of their passage refunded.

In September 1941 William George Hynard at the Board of Trade wrote to both companies asking whether they would be prepared to participate in the plan. Positive responses were immediate and by the end of the month arrangements were in place. All Americans considered to be suitable for a commission in the Royal Navy received the following letter from Philip Edward Marrack, head of Commissions and Warrants, who was involved in organizing the procedure. Written in prize English prose made tactfully elliptic, it is typical understatement from the country they were about to fight for:

> Collumpton Highfield
> Ashstead, Surrey, England
> Dear ____
> I write to tell you that if you will come to England about [date] I think you will be able to find employment. You should visit one of the agents of either the Cunard Company or the Canadian Pacific Company in Canada. Show them this letter and arrange with them to come to England on one of their vessels. On arrival in England you should show this letter to the Immigration Authorities. You should come to London, call at 50 Queen Anne Gate, S.W.1 and ask for Mr. Hoffman who would tell you where to go.

The Queen Anne Gate address housed a branch of Britain's Foreign Office.

Shipping companies received copies of the form letter, and were advised that the volunteers did not need passports as arrangements were in hand with immigration authorities in the United Kingdom to ensure a seamless entry into the country. Utmost secrecy was strongly emphasized. Unfortunately, in spite of facilitating the passage of volunteers, by June 1940, the Royal Navy had not secured the services of any American volunteers for its Fleet Air Arm, besides Taylor. Something more had to be done.

The Admiralty told Lord Lothian, Britain's ambassador in Washington, that Taylor was being sent to New York ostensibly to deal with technical matters but also to try and secure, as quickly as possible, the services of experienced U.S. Navy pilots willing to join the Royal Navy. Applicants were directed to proceed to Ottawa to have their records examined by the Canadian navy for possible further assignment to the RNVR, pending resignation of their U.S. military commissions. The ambassador was asked to advance money for volunteers and to consider whether the arrangements were likely to provoke any political complications in the United States. His answer shows that there was a sizeable pro-British lobby in the U.S. government that was willing to help Britain get its American volunteers.

Lothian wrote:

> I have learnt that the State Department informed the Canadian legation some four weeks ago "on highest authority" that it would not cause embarrassment to the United States authorities if American citizens were to proceed to Canada to enlist in the Canadian forces. Presumably we can take it that it would equally cause no embarrassment to United States authorities if these American citizens subsequently proceeded through "combat area" to the United Kingdom in defiance of the provisions of the Neutrality Act. In view of this communication from the State Department I think that we can now regard ourselves as being given a fairly free hand to encourage Americans to volunteer for service in the British armed forces provided always that actual enlistment is not effected in this country. (File ADM 1/11259)

The U.S. military was kept informed and the whole business was thinly disguised. Lothian concluded his letter with the observation,

> I see no reason why Lieutenant Taylor should not act as suggested provided he gives no interviews. He ought not . . . actually enlist anyone in this country or make any advances of pay or traveling expenses to potential volunteers. All he should do is to let it be known to his friends possessing necessary qualifications that if they care to volunteer they will be very welcome and can obtain further details if they proceed to Canada where their traveling expenses will be refunded. It is possible . . . that some difficulty may arise if the United States Navy Department are reluctant to allow pilots in their Reserve to resign their American commissions. Naval Attaché is making enquiries as to probable attitude of Navy Department in this connection and we will be guided by what they say in giving advice on his arrival.

Taylor recruited no one. The U.S. Navy needed every aviator in its inventory and the Army Air Corps was equally strapped for pilots. Claire Chennault had exhausted the pool of scarce pilots with his volunteers for the Chinese air force.

In February 1941, Lend-Lease legislation passed in the House of Representatives by a vote of 260 to 165 and a month later the Senate voted 60 to 31 in favor. By this act the United States made fifty old destroyers available in exchange for ninety-nine-year base rights in Britain's colonial possessions. At the Admiralty, Philip Marrack quickly calculated that the manning needs to ferry the U.S. warships to Britain required the Royal Navy to find many extra trained officers, more than were easily available from existing manpower reserves. He recommended that if American officers assigned as crew during the transfer of ships volunteered for the Royal Navy, their services should be accepted. By early July, London's Foreign Office notified Lord Lothian in Washington of the Admiralty's decision that American naval deck officers who could be found—provided they were fit for sea and had recent service experience—would be welcome in the Royal Navy.

The Admiralty needed men who could be trained as seagoing officers but their intake needed to be governed by available space in training facilities, and as the training was short the candidates had to be technically qualified. The eligibility pool included Merchant Marine officers as well as experienced yachtsmen capable of navigating and performing general, unrestricted line officer duties with minimal instruction. Other naval branches—engineering officers, for example—were required to have a university degree or equivalent qualification together with a minimum of one year of practical experience. Deck officers mostly needed to know ship handling. The maximum age limit was set at twenty-eight. The Foreign Office suggested to Lord Lothian that candidates should be sent to Halifax, Nova Scotia, for entry but before sending them it would be necessary to ensure the men were suited for military service. The Navy Department would be asked to give advice on character and qualification screening. The Admiralty was willing to send an officer to Washington to assist in the selection process.

The Foreign Office also wanted Lothian to follow up an offer by Belle Roosevelt, Theodore Roosevelt's daughter-in-law, to arrange for Americans to help the war effort. Specifically, would she cooperate in collecting the names of officers and arranging for their transit to Halifax? Mrs. Roosevelt's interest, "the terms of which have been sent, we understand, with the connivance of high authority," indicated she was willing to arrange for U.S. citizens to proceed to England via Canada. Reference to "high authority" probably meant the sitting president in the White House. There was Roosevelt family precedence for service in an English uniform. Unwilling to wait for America's entry into World War I, Belle's husband, Kermit, fought with the British army in the Middle East and published an account of his experience titled *War in the Garden of Eden*. After August 1917, when the United States came into World War I, he joined the American Expeditionary Force in France. Kermit served again briefly with the British army in World War II before the attack on Pearl Harbor, later taking a commission in the U.S. Army.

Others in His Majesty's government were quick to recognize the public relations benefit of putting Americans in British uniform. (Later, Sir) David Scott, head of the consular section at the Foreign Office, declared that while Mrs. Roosevelt's offer was "satisfactory as far as it goes we are strongly of the opinion that we should go considerably further" (ibid.). Scott readily acknowledged that London was effectively debarred from authorizing Lothian to cheer Mrs. Roosevelt's recruiting within the United States, and that there were also military reasons behind the War Office's view that it was in the sphere of materiél—rather than personnel—that assistance from the United States would be most welcomed. However, there were overriding pragmatic political reasons that made it unwise to have too rigid a standpoint.

The advertising value of Americans in British uniform was immense. Scott was among the first to articulate what became British policy during the twenty-six months of America's neutrality. He was unabashedly in favor of exploiting the publicity and flatly said, "We have to remember that as matters now stand every American enlisting in the armed forces of the Crown is worth his weight in gold to us as a propagandist, and that from the point of view of influencing United States opinion in our favor there is everything to be said for encouraging as many United States citizens as possible to join our forces" (ibid.).

The age limit of twenty-eight was completely ignored; otherwise, fewer than half of the American RNVR officers would have made the cut. Hayes and Kauffman missed the cutoff by about a year. Buck, Cherry, Deiter, Hampson, Hoague, Kittridge, Leggat, Porter, Ripley, Russell, and Taylor were all in their thirties. Konow was forty-one. At fifty-one, Parker holds the record. He exceeded the British age limit by more than twenty years.

Lothian's answer was an accurate prediction of the outcome of a recruiting campaign in the United States. He cabled his response:

> I fear that it is unlikely that any appreciable number of American naval officers, naval engineers or men with naval experience will wish to volunteer for service with the Royal Navy. I am however about to issue a notice to the press giving details about those British subjects resident in this country who will be welcome for service in the Royal Navy, and as a result some Americans, especially yachtsmen may volunteer. I will furthermore do my best to arrange to make it known discreetly that Americans with the qualifications mentioned in your telegram will be welcome. I have also arranged for Lieutenant Taylor to approach Mrs. Kermit Roosevelt in the matter. Lieutenant Taylor, RNVR, thought she might be able to interest a certain number of yachtsmen but I am not altogether optimistic. (ibid.)

Lothian recognized the legal pitfalls at once and also advised that it would be a mistake to approach the U.S. Navy. U.S. naval authorities he thought, "would be embarrassed to connive at something which almost amounts to a breach of the law in respect of recruiting in the United States, and they might well resent it if they thought we were endeavoring to secure the services of ex–naval personnel or men suitable for naval employment at a time when the American Navy is being greatly increased and reservists called up. It might however be possible to consult with the Navy Department privately about the qualifications of any individuals who actually volunteer" (ibid.). He added, rightly, that it would be indiscreet to send a British naval officer to Washington to assist in the selection of American candidates.

Months passed without result.

Mrs. Roosevelt's organization, it was clear, would not undertake the selection of volunteers. No doubt she meant well but the issue extended well beyond her social reach. By August 1940 arrangements had still not been made for the reception of Americans for the Royal Navy in Canada. The matter was particularly urgent because help was needed to ferry the leased destroyers to the United Kingdom. In October the director of Naval Intelligence noted that selection of officers would be carried out on the recommendation of the consuls in respect of each volunteer's character and fitness. Despite the procedures put in place, by late autumn the Royal Navy had not managed to recruit a single American deck officer under the plan. Impatience was beginning to show.

Philip Marrack's enthusiasm had cooled considerably when he wrote testily "naval Attaché is not producing any recruits, but not proposed to press him as they [the recruits] may well be more trouble than they are worth." The situation worsened after Lothian died unexpectedly in late December 1940. The consulate in New York as well as the embassy in Washington, unaccountably, became obstacles to eager volunteers, as Edward Ferris, John Parker, and Charles Porter found out.

In time, Marrack softened and he actually helped to solve the problem by having the candidates present themselves in Halifax where they would be transferred directly to the Royal Navy. However, Canada was nervous about letting its territory be used for the purpose. To mollify these misgivings it was suggested that Canada be allowed to supervise the process. The Second Sea Lord disagreed. If Americans volunteered to serve as officers in the Royal Navy it could be done, he insisted, without offending anyone in Canada by enlisting the help of Rear Admiral (later, Vice Admiral Sir) Stuart S. Bonham-Carter, RN, KCB, CVO, DSO, the commander Escort Force, Halifax, Nova Scotia, and coordinator of convoy protection to the United Kingdom. It was an inspired solution. In North America, Halifax became the principal conduit used by U.S. citizens who were hell-bent on joining the Royal Navy.

Parker had tried the U.S. Navy in summer 1940. He made a trip across Boston Harbor to the Charleston Navy Yard, not necessarily to seek a commission because he was indifferent to rank, but simply to go back to life in a warship at a time of national peril. Keenness alone cannot qualify a man over the age of fifty for military service and the officer in charge of enlistments shook his head.

Undeterred, Parker took himself north to the border and tried to get into the Black Watch of Canada. Predictably, his half-century age was against him and he was turned down. It is unlikely that his heart was ever in being a kilted infantryman, anyway. Parker was a sailor, through and through. He next turned to the Royal Navy when word reached him that Britain wanted experienced yachtsmen as naval officers. It was the hoped-for cue. He called on Mr. Ford, the British Consul in Boston, who directed him to apply at the

British Embassy in Washington, D.C. Thus began a frustrating odyssey of travels, contradictory instructions, and the sort of stony but polite indifference in which bureaucrats excel.

The consul had not heard about, or was unwilling to bother with, implementing arrangements that allowed British consulates to accept American citizens for service in His Majesty's forces. Parker got assurance from the naval attaché in Washington, D.C., Rear Admiral Herbert Pott, that he would be contacted when "certain legal obstacles were overcome" (Parker statement to Admiralty, 30 June 1941, Judith Parker papers). Parker's friends Porter, also from Boston, and Ferris of New York City received the same treatment. The three joined forces.

Parker described the whole episode:

> About the middle of April [1941], not having heard from the naval attaché and Ford having no information, Porter, Ferris and I consulted and decided that I should go to Halifax where Rear Admiral Stuart Bonham-Carter was evidently very anxious to help. Bonham-Carter expressed surprise that we had not heard from our local British Consuls or from Admiral Pott. I showed him a personal letter from Under Secretary of State Sumner Welles stating that Americans would not lose their citizenship on joining Canadian or British forces provided they did so in Canada, but were liable to punishment if they went into the war zone. I made it clear that Porter, Ferris and myself were willing to take the risk of such punishment. Bonham-Carter telephoned Pott in my presence asking if he could not take us in Canada and was told it was impossible, but that the whole matter was in train and it would be a very short time before we could apply to our local British consulates. About May 1, having heard nothing I got a friend in our State Department to call the naval attaché but Admiral Pott told him there had been a further delay. (Judith Parker papers)

In a classic example of bureaucratic stonewalling, the consul in New York, Mr. G. Haggard, and the one in Boston, Mr. Ford, politely offered to keep a list of the names of American volunteers, make immediate inquiries and get at a prompt resolution and the like. By all traceable accounts they did nothing. Nothing, that is, until officials in Whitehall, the Admiralty, and elsewhere in London's senior political circles determined that it was to England's best advantage to have citizens of neutral America in the Royal Navy.

Edward Ferris now took his turn to make the journey to Halifax. Like some of the other Americans who went into British military ranks, he first tried to become a U.S. Navy officer but his age was a barrier and he was rejected for a commission. When he had at last succeeded in being accepted by the Royal Navy, a London newspaper with a flair for tabloid sensationalism described a cliffhanger. The story went that Ferris had crossed the border into Canada to volunteer the night before he was due to be drafted into the U.S. Army. The facts were rather less colorful. In truth, British civilian officialdom on either side of the border had been the formidable obstacles.

Over a period of ten weeks Ferris traveled repeatedly between New York City, Boston, Montreal, and Ottawa entirely at his own expense in a single-minded pursuit of the King's commission. He petitioned for acceptance and followed one blind alley after another. He made no less than eight visits to the British Consul General in Manhattan, all fruitless. The U.S.-based diplomatic side of Great Britain's official relationship with the United States was indifferent, even hostile. It stuck to an attitude of stubborn denial that anything at all could be done to facilitate the entry of any qualified American into the Royal Navy.

In Halifax Ferris met Bonham-Carter. Considerably in advance of Haggard and Ford (or in spite of them) Bonham-Carter had from early on encouraged suitable American applicants. Ferris, like Parker and Porter, was a businessman who also had yachting credentials. Socially and intellectually the men fit the profile of candidates who could be screened quickly for approval. Age was not made a barrier; although Parker was obviously far too old he created a transparent and easily debunked fiction about his birth date. Bonham-Carter did not care about trifles: he wanted qualified officers. Congenial, gracious, and immensely capable he came to understand how difficult things were being made for these American recruits and simply "got on with things," as Ferris explained.

Once inside the Admiral's domain and after the usual office call Ferris was asked only if he would be prepared to stay if accepted. As he was already packed and ready to sail he agreed at once. He was now at the end of an odyssey that began in March. After passing a medical exam Ferris was commissioned a lieutenant in mid-May 1941. The following day he reported aboard HMS *Sennen*, a converted ex–U.S. Coast Guard cutter. He immediately cabled Parker and Porter who arrived in Halifax the next day. On June 7 Bonham-Carter commissioned Parker as a (Temporary) Lieutenant, RNVR. Parker gave his age as forty. There was still time to buy a smart new uniform and for Violet to come up from Boston and say good-bye. Porter was with them and took a snapshot of the couple, their last photograph together, in the city's Public Garden.

Charles Burnham Porter was the third man to arrive at Greenwich. In 1939, at the outbreak of war in Europe he, too, had attempted to join the U.S. Navy but failed his physical exam. As others discovered, less than perfect eyesight was unacceptable for the unrestricted line duties of a warship's deck officer. Porter quickly switched directions and made his aim the Royal Navy. With Ferris and Parker he spent months running between Washington, Boston, and Halifax trying mightily to be let in. On June 19, 1941, Bonham-Carter gave Porter his wish. Porter was the last of the trio to be commissioned. For the Atlantic crossing the Royal Navy put him aboard HMS *Repulse*, a *Renown*-class battle cruiser which a month earlier had taken part in the pursuit of Germany's *Bismarck*. Just six months later *Repulse* was attacked and sunk by Japanese aircraft off Malaya. Porter landed in the United Kingdom at Greenock, Scotland. Once in London, like most of the volunteers, he reported to the Royal Naval College, Greenwich, for training.

Ferris, Parker, and Porter (in that order) were the first three U.S. citizen volunteers to report to the college and it was their arrival that inspired the plaque that was placed in the floor of the Painted Hall.

In marked contrast to the travails experienced by Parker and company, Kauffman was amazed by the speed of acceptance and trust he encountered in an England that was already heavily under siege and highly security conscious. He could not imagine a foreigner being made an officer in the U.S. Navy in the brief span between breakfast and an early dinner.

The Royal Navy sent him for training to HMS *King Alfred* at Hove near the Sussex seaside town of Brighton, making him one of the few volunteers who did not go to Greenwich. His training experience was not any different from what the others experienced. HMS *King Alfred* was a dedicated RNVR training base, and once it had opened most wartime trainees passed through it rather than Greenwich. There were two types of wartime trainees: commissioned warrant candidates who came through the lower rank with a minimum of three months' sea time and the "Y" scheme, which directly recruited educationally qualified young men with officer potential. Draper Kauffman would have been placed under the "Y" scheme. Kauffman described the ten-week course as "excellent, very well run and I was very happy there although they did have some Special Branch [civilian police] people involved, it was primarily about training RNVR officers to be junior officers at sea. They did a superb job, for instance, on indoctrination into the Royal Navy. Not stuffy. People might think that it would be, but it wasn't at all—the history of the Royal Navy, that you should be darned proud to wear the uniform and that sort of thing. They did magnificently well" (USNI Oral History Program, May 1978 interview, transcript provided by Mrs. Barbara Kauffman Bush).

At Greenwich, Parker experienced difficulty understanding the British fashion of teaching, its terminology and style and methods, but found it easier going after settling in and making friends.

Gibson remembered "the Captain of the College, during my time [Captain John Cecil Davis] particularly, and the splendors of taking all meals and guest nights in the extraordinary Painted Hall" (correspondence, Eric Gibson collection). The Hall is so named for its mass of splendid murals. Diners sit at long, polished wooden tables replete with rows of gleaming silver candelabra. The atmosphere is elegant and formal and altogether grand.

The college watched its charges carefully and had a sharp eye for talent. They soon found that Ferris was a natural leader and born naval officer. His innate qualities of quiet confidence, steadiness of temperament, and modest demeanor got high marks. He inspired subordinates to do their best, and he encouraged superiors to pile on greater responsibilities. Ferris impressed both the college faculty and the Admiralty who made him a first lieutenant on his initial assignment. First lieutenant in the Royal Navy, informally called Number One, is the second in command who ranks next to the ship's captain. Ferris' orders sent him to HMS *Sennen*, the same ex–U.S. Coast Guard ship that had brought him to England from Canada.

Alex Henry Cherry loved it all. "I had never looked at [Drake and Raleigh] as British but almost as though they were the earliest forerunners of what was later to become Americans," he exclaimed. It was Churchill's famous words, "I have nothing to offer but blood, toil, sweat and tears . . . Let us go forward together with our united strength . . . we shall fight on the beaches, we shall fight on the landing grounds, we shall fight in the fields and in the streets . . . we shall never surrender," that galvanized Cherry. He was especially taken by the "we shall never surrender" part. Cherry "waited no longer." Fortunately, those who went before him had blazed a way through the bureaucratic wilderness, and he encountered no remaining obstacle to his goal.

At the British consulate's office on Broadway in Manhattan, there were formalities to complete and an introduction arranged. Then Cherry left to pack his bags—and his ukulele—to make his way to Halifax. The half-hour interview with Bonham-Carter ended with a schooner of sherry and "some pleasant conversation."

Cherry was commissioned and berthed aboard the battleship HMS *Malaya* sailing for Rosyth, Scotland. With *Malaya* at the time of the transit was Commander C. R. Purse, OBE, DSC and bar, RN, who reminisced:

> During the passage from Halifax to Scapa Flow, four of us, including Alex, were playing ordinary Auction Bridge for the usual two pennies a hundred. Suddenly, the numerous destroyers who were escorting *Malaya* thought they had detected a German submarine on their ASDIC instruments. They immediately attacked the contact, which was probably fish, with many depth charges. The noise and explosions were terrific and *Malaya* shuddered frequently. We RN officers were quite used to these occurrences and there was nothing we could do about it, anyway, and we continued to bid "three Hearts" on "four Spades" above the noise and din. Poor Alex, who was not used to this sort of thing and was becoming more and more agitated, forgot to go "Five Hearts" although he had a grand slam in his hand and finally threw down his cards saying "How the devil can you fellows play cards with death and destruction going on all around you?" Needless to say he was my partner at the time! (Cherry correspondence, Michael Sabatell collection)

From Scotland Cherry took the train to London. He expected the Admiralty to send him immediately to a warship to fight the enemy, but like the others he was ordered to the Royal Naval College. The thought flashed in his mind, "It is the year 1941 and a new foe threatened Britain with invasion. I couldn't help chuckling to myself: And this time I'm here to help." Among his early priorities after settling in was to write a letter to Franklin D. Roosevelt: "Dear Mr. President, I've done what you really wanted, I've joined Nelson's Navy. I'm backing your foreign policy to the nth degree" (ibid.). There is no record of a White House reply. Joining the Royal Navy is not exactly what Roosevelt was advocating at that time, but Cherry's high spirits cannot be doubted.

"What was the [Atlantic] crossing like?" the commander of the college wanted to know.

Cherry answered, "I was informed the journey was without incident if one makes allowances for depth-charge attacks, reports of the [German battleship] *Scharnhorst* looking for our convoy and being flung out of bed by nocturnal gun practice."

"What made you join?" continued the commander.

"Well, sir, we had a very poor grouse season back home," came the answer. As an American citizen Cherry attracted a lot of attention and often got the same kind of questions from others. "Thought you were a Canadian," an officer told him. "Never imagined an American with us. Jolly good. What made you come?"

"Well, I had an insatiable desire to see where Shakespeare is buried. Do you know of a better way of taking a holiday?" replied Cherry.

He readily picked up the British idioms of his day like "jolly decent," "bloody well," "the blokes," and "cheerio" but never forgot to remind anyone who might have been in doubt that he was an American—not a Canadian—and he relished the attention. "New here! Joining us?" a college instructor barked. "So new I can still taste Aunt Jemima's buckwheat cakes," he promptly replied. Cherry recalled seeing Parker write a letter to his family in Boston the night before Parker joined HMS *Broadwater* in Liverpool. Cherry's book *Yankee RN* was dedicated to Parker.

The Americans came to Britain at the most dismal time in the country's history. They were a tiny minority that was to swell in the coming months with the arrival of many more of their countrymen. At the new plaque's dedication ceremonies in 2001, Winston Churchill's grandson said of the volunteers, "Their numbers may not have been great, but the fact that they came, at a moment when Britain stood alone, meant so much. They proved to be the harbingers of the millions that were to come later."

The narration in a wartime film, *A Canterbury Tale*, regaled the audience with a series of tongue-in-cheek facts and figures. We learn that there were 10 million men and women in U.S. Armed Forces during World War II. Three million served in the European theater of operations and of that number 2.5 million were stationed in England. Half of them liked it, the other half didn't. Of those who did like England, three-fourths liked the pubs; one-fourth liked the girls; one-tenth liked modern English literature; one one-hundredth liked the classics; one one-thousandth liked the historic buildings; one ten-thousandth liked the old churches, and of this latter group two-thirds wanted to revisit England after the war.

It was an England that was culturally unprepared for them. Compared to the United States, the Great Britain of the day remained much closer to the previous Victorian century. The stratified British social system did not always mesh easily with the free-wheeling ways of Americans who were oblivious to class distinctions, and who would often glide over sensibilities they were unaware had been ruffled.

G. K. Chesterton observed that tradition represented "the democracy of the dead" and things had, indeed, been slow to change in prewar Britain. The rush of Americans brushed away many of the remaining vestiges of the nineteenth century. *Time* magazine reporter Lael Laird noted that locals and visitors regarded one another with bemusement, sometimes with bewilderment and always with a sense of their clear differences in manner, dress, and speech and in their respective methods of doing business. Ancient patterns and attitudes were challenged when streetwise Brooklyn met the older culture and social deference took a beating ("Yanks in England," *Time*, 17 July 1942).

Throughout Britain, young Americans looked in the wrong direction for traffic, crowded under the low ceilings of country pubs with unfamiliar names like Carpenter's Arms, Black Friars, Red Lion, Black Horse, and Bull and Bushes. They drove confidently and fast in their jeeps, roller-coasting along narrow, sunken, and sharply twisting rural lanes. All over a tiny "green and pleasant land" walled gardens opened and old houses came alive to the new arrivals. Teatime was no longer sacred. Yanks surprised a population that had only Hollywood impressions of what Americans were supposed to be like. Local chefs catered to U.S. tastes: coleslaw, peanut butter, and ketchup on practically everything, even on scrambled eggs. People tsk-tsked that Yanks eat only with their fork. The coffee got better. Historical perspectives were challenged. One American reported with genuine incredulity: "You know what they teach kids in this country? They teach them that England won the last war! [World War I] Can you beat that? It's a fact. A couple of little kids told me so themselves" (Lael Laird, *Time,* 27 July 1942).

Brock McElheran remembered the city teeming with uniforms of all commonwealth services, and Americans galore, alongside gallant men and women who had escaped from the continent. Walking along any sidewalk in the West End, the theater district, one jostled against majors in the "Grenadier Guards, Canadian army nurses, wing commanders in the Royal Australian Air Force, captains of the Fighting French, stokers wearing HMS on their sailor caps (ships were never named), sergeant pilots from Bomber Command, [an alphabet soup of] WRNS, WAAFs, and WAACs, women in khaki from artillery batteries, beribboned rear admirals," aircraftsmen second class from the Royal New Zealand Air Force, and ruddy-complexioned young women from the Land Army. No one had ever seen the like (Brock McElheran, *V-Bombs and Weathermaps*, Quebec: McGill-Queen's University Press, 1995).

In time the U.S. Navy set up its European Command headquarters across the square from the U.S. Embassy. Commander Alfred Stanford, USNR, remembered "The [ticket] clippies on the Oxford Street bus shouted importantly to their passengers to make way as an American naval officer struggled through the crowd" to get off at Audley Street, to walk the couple blocks to 20 Grosvenor Square (Alfred Stanford, *Force Mulberry*, Whitehead Press, 2007).

When London's *Daily Express* newspaper printed a box, "Take an American Soldier Home to Tea on July 4th," a long line of Britons formed to extend invitations. Americans and their English counterparts crowded the same corner pubs, groused about prices, and jostled each other in Piccadilly Circus and Trafalgar Square. When a baseball mound was built in Wembley Stadium for a game between two U.S. service teams, the *Times* informed readers "its use adds to the speed of throw." In Hyde Park, softball became an evening ritual where civilians gathered enthusiastically and cheered in the wrong places. It was joked that so much chewing gum (not an English habit back then) had been thrown down in Trafalgar Square the "pigeons there were said to be laying rubber eggs." Mint humbugs made room for Hershey chocolate bars. Americans altered much about the way England listened to music (particularly dance bands) and how they dressed and thought.

The Royal Navy's Americans liked Britain and Britain cheerfully reciprocated. The volunteers admired England's brave spirit in the face of appalling odds, and they liked the island's way of life. Kauffman said he could not buy a beer when pub customers heard a Yankee accent come from a Royal Navy uniform: people competed with each other to treat him to a pint. Generosity became overwhelming if anyone caught a glimpse of his car, which was marked as a vehicle assigned to bomb disposal personnel. Russell was welcomed and accepted at Blenheim Palace. People at all levels were moved by the Americans' willingness to pitch in with them, and slightly astonished they would want to do so freely, of their own accord.

Between his Royal Naval College studies Parker socialized with his son Frank whose regiment had arrived from Canada. They met at London's Cavendish Hotel to enjoy the owner's famous hospitality. The "Duchess of Jermyn Street," Rosa Lewis, had worked her way up to become head of a duke's kitchen where she mastered French cuisine. With a glowing reputation for her private catering she won the patronage of the future king, Edward VII. By 1902 Rosa had put aside the means to buy her own hotel and ran it as a kind of exclusive club. Her biographer, Michael Harrison, wrote that "all the accepted visitors, regular or irregular, seemed to know each other. Outsiders not frozen by a look from R. L. never stayed long." Rosa's hospitality was boundless and her business methods unorthodox. "Whoever she thought had the most money got the bill for all the champagne cocktails, which he either never paid, or paid with a dud cheque." Rosa's catchphrase was "People only come to the Cavendish to bounce cheques and pee!" (Harrison, *Rosa*, London: Peter Davies, 1962). She adored John and his son and gave them all sorts of special privileges, including unlimited credit. During the last months of his father's life Frank and his father met at the hotel and got to know one another in an entirely new way. As adults they shared a common goal and the same ethical convictions about the enemy and the reasons for the conflict. Frank had a strong sense that his father expected to die in the war, but they never spoke of it.

Reaction to John's death was instant and heartfelt. For Rosa, Parker's loss was "too deep for words. It is the same to me as if I had lost my own child. He was a man who would never grow up. So eager to do all he could for everybody. So full of life himself and a true life-giver. A brave man" (correspondence, 29 October 1941, Judith Parker papers). Rear Admiral Herbert Pott wrote to the family about a tribute published in the *Times*, "[John's] . . . coming over here and as an American being killed in action as a British Naval Officer is an inspiring example of Anglo-American comradeship" (Judith Parker papers). At the Royal Naval College, Commander Charles Pitcairn-Jones, RN, spoke for all when he said:

> Those citizens of the United States who came over when things were looking more than a bit dubious made the deepest impression. . . . I cannot express my feelings on the subject properly. It wasn't only the encouragement they gave by their act of faith at a time when it must have seemed that the issue was very uncertain; nor was it gratitude for the sympathy they were showing in such a practical manner. To me at least there was something more than that . . . the real fact of the matter was that they obviously felt that the things worth fighting for were, on the whole the right things. It makes a very strong bond when one believes that the things that are so sacred that one hardly ever speaks of them are understood and shared. Those . . . who saw fit to become Sea Officers of the Royal Navy just at that time meant a great deal to us and touched feelings that I cannot express in words—feelings far deeper than those occasioned by anything afterwards. (ibid.)

15th JUNE 1941
On this day came three citizens of
THE UNITED STATES OF AMERICA
The first of their countrymen to become Sea-Officers of
THE ROYAL NAVY

The plaque set in the floor of Painted Hall, Royal Naval College, Greenwich, in 1941. (R. E. White collection)

Captain John Cecil Davis, OBE, captain of the College (right) and Commander John Rochfort D'Oyly-Carte, commander of the College (the second in command) had the plaque set in the Painted Hall, where this photograph was taken. The WRNS officer is Sybil Sassoon, Marchioness of Cholmondeley, CBE, who became the wartime superintendent of the Women's Royal Naval Service. (June and John Wallace collection)

On bridge watch the night of October 17–18 was Lieutenant John Stanley Parker. He had confided in a letter to his wife, "I'm doing exactly what I was made for, in what I have always wanted. . . . Doing what has to be done and all I'm fit for any more." Parker is the second U.S. volunteer indicated by the plaque in the Painted Hall, Royal Naval College. He was the oldest volunteer and the first to die. (Parker family collection)

Edward Mortimer Ferris aboard HMS Sennen. *He was the first man to report to the Royal Naval College, Greenwich. The faculty gave him high marks for leadership. For his initial posting he was appointed* Sennen's *first lieutenant. (Ken Reed collection)*

Charles Burnham Porter was the third American to arrive at Royal Naval College, Greenwich. His wartime assignment was to the staff of commander in chief, The Nore where he worked eighty feet belowground near the entrance to the River Thames. (U.S. Navy)

Edmund Webster Kittredge (center) aboard the light cruiser HMS Diomede *deployed in the South Atlantic. He later became a beach commando and was wounded during the invasion of Sicily, Operation Husky. (Kittredge family collection)*

Nicknamed "The Leaping Dane," Carl Konow was the scion of a Danish family with a distinguished naval past. He was an immigrant to the United States where he hoped to make a career in aviation. Konow participated in the invasions of Sicily and Normandy and commanded HM LST 198. *(Konow family collection)*

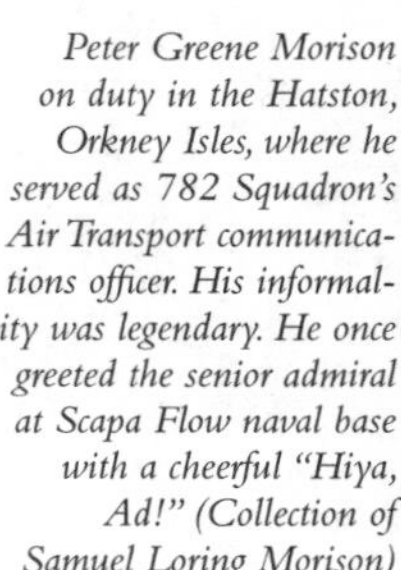

Peter Greene Morison on duty in the Hatston, Orkney Isles, where he served as 782 Squadron's Air Transport communications officer. His informality was legendary. He once greeted the senior admiral at Scapa Flow naval base with a cheerful "Hiya, Ad!" (Collection of Samuel Loring Morison)

The Royal Navy made David Gibson a destroyer sailor. He participated in the Normandy invasion and commanded three Lend-Lease ships on their return to the United States. (Eric Gibson collection)

Rear Admiral (later, Vice Admiral Sir) Stuart S. Bonham-Carter, the affable and competent Royal Navy commander in Halifax who had no qualms about commissioning any qualified U.S. citizen who wished to serve in the Royal Navy. (Imperial War Museum)

The new plaque with all the names, dedicated in 2001. Francis Hayes was the last officer to be found. (Photo by Joe Greaves-Lord)

The Old Royal Naval College, Greenwich, where Britannia trained her officers in naval science from 1873 to 1998. (Copyright James Brittain. Published with permission of the Greenwich Foundation)

Battle of the Atlantic

The Battle of the Atlantic lasted for the duration of the war—almost six years—from the declaration of war on September 3, 1939, to May 4, 1945, when Grand Admiral Dönitz ordered his fleet of U-boats to stand down. It was the longest continuing fight of World War II, perhaps of any war in history. Engagements occurred most heavily along the shipping routes between North America and the European Allies in every navigable ocean, sea, strait, gulf, and bay across hundreds of thousands of square miles of blue water. From autumn 1939 until the United States was attacked by Japan and joined the Allies, there was a gap of twenty-seven months in which Kriegsmarine U-boats prosecuted a virtual siege in the North Atlantic against the resupply of England. Despite implementation of the convoy system, antisubmarine resources, tactics, and measures were inadequate to prevent catastrophic losses. Food, fuel, and material imports to the United Kingdom were reduced by nearly half. People became hungry; clothes looked tired, over-worn. The government introduced rationing of food, clothes, and petrol. Life took on a sallow aspect.

Even more devastating was the sense that Britain lay helpless, encircled by a virtually unstoppable, invisible menace that was slowly starving the population to death. The psychological dread had a deeply negative mental effect on the population. Even with the horrendous effects of the Blitz in mind, Prime Minister Winston Churchill wrote, "The only thing that really frightened me during the war was the U-boat peril." Slowly, things changed for the better. The U.S. Navy's chief of naval operations, Admiral Ernest King's, reluctance to introduce the convoy system was overcome. Sonar was derived from ASDIC, a

British invention during the First World War; the Enigma code was broken by British and Polish code breakers at Bletchley Park; the Leigh Light came into service in 1942; and radar, which was developed simultaneously in a number of countries, was installed everywhere. The first escort carrier was HMS *Audacity*. America introduced advanced production techniques for warship and Merchant Navy construction, as well as aircraft, materiél in unprecedented quantities, epic quantities of track and wheeled vehicles, and sixteen million men under arms between 1941 and 1945.

The Battle of the Atlantic (the name originated with Churchill) was not a single clash of arms but a series of individual battles and skirmishes among submarines, surface ships, and aircraft. The fearful toll in lives, ships sunk, and cargo lost staggers the imagination. The Allies paid with 30,000 sailors killed; about the same number of German sailors died. Some 4,000 merchant ships and warships were sunk, including over 700 U-boats. The effort exhausted body and soul. When victory in Europe was finally achieved, the Allies instructed all German submarines still deployed on combat duty to make themselves visibly distinctive and radio their positions.

Nicholas Monsarrat wrote the most vivid description of what happened next:

> All over the broad Atlantic, wherever they had been working or lying hid, the U-boats surfaced, confessing the war's end . . . they hoisted their black flags, and said where they were, and waited for orders. They rose, dripping and silent, in the Irish Sea, and at the mouth of the Clyde, and off the Lizard in the English Channel, and at the top of the Minches where the tides raced; they rose near Iceland and off the northwest tip of Ireland, and close to the Faroes, and on the Gibraltar run where the ships lay so thick, and near St. John's and Halifax, and in the deep of the Atlantic, with three thousand fathoms of water beneath their keel. They surfaced in secret places, betraying themselves and their frustrated plans: they rose within sight of land, they rose far away in mortal waters where, on the map of the battle, the crosses that were sunken ships were etched so many and so close that the ink ran together. (*The Cruel Sea*, London: The Reprint Society, 1953)

The anger and dread in his tone is easy to understand. In 1940 the average sinking per U-boat per month was 60,000 tons.

More than half the American volunteers participated in some manner in the Battle of the Atlantic: Parker, Cherry, Gibson, Deiter, Ferris, Porter, Kittredge, Leggat, Homans, Lee, Hayes, Russell, Ripley, Stilwell, Taylor, and van Epps. Edward Ferris' first posting, as first lieutenant in HMS *Sennen*, brought him convoy escort service between the United Kingdom and West Africa. He later served on the small ex-French destroyer HMS *La Melpomene*, commissioned into the Royal Navy against the wishes of the French government and of the crew. The opposition is rooted in a lasting bitterness.

On July 3, 1940, following the armistice signed by France's Petain and Hitler, the Royal Navy destroyed France's Atlantic Fleet anchored in Mers el Kebir. The attack came after negotiations for deployment of the French warships broke down. The British wanted France to join with the Royal Navy, sink or disable the ships, or sail them to the French West Indies, all to avoid them falling under German control. A hapless series of misunderstandings, bruised egos, and cultural differences wrecked discussions. More than 1,200 French sailors were killed and 350 wounded by the British attack, which was personally ordered by Churchill. The incident sent a signal to other countries, particularly the United States, that Britain was prepared to fight with utter ruthlessness if necessary. The incident marks a signal moment in the fate of the French navy and of the French Republic. It left a deep national scar that has never fully healed. British sailors, mostly without trouble, seized all French ships that were in British ports at that time, *La Melpomene* among them. An officer and a rating were killed in Plymouth boarding the submarine *Surcouf* when its crew resisted.

Promoted to lieutenant commander, Ferris took command of the frigate escort HMS *Byard* (ex–USS *Donaldson*) on patrol in the North Atlantic. He was already on board and had participated in the sinking of *U-841* when he was tapped for command. *Byard* was the first Captain-class frigate to score a U-boat sinking. *Byard*'s battle honors are for North Atlantic service but according to Ferris' widow, Kathleen Parry, *Byard* was detached to escort troops and ships—specifically landing craft—to Allied forces invading Italy. In the harbor at Anzio a bomb burst on the bridge, destroying Ferris' sight in one eye and impairing his vision in the other.

He had taken command in January 1944, just before the beachhead assault. Reporting his injuries would have meant loss of command. Ferris managed to hide his condition and carry on until June, but once informed, Royal Navy physicians ordered him home. Ferris' sight was so poor that he had to be assisted ashore. It says something about the measure of Ferris' leadership that the crew, officers, and ratings kept his injuries secret. After treatment he attended the senior officers course at Greenwich, the only one of the volunteers to do so, and graduated in highest place. His daughter, Penni, was born while he was enrolled in the course.

The black crosses were being applied to the map at a great pace in mid-October 1941, when HMS *Broadwater* put to sea with its aging American lieutenant on board. The ship was not much improved beyond its original World War I U.S. Navy capabilities except her armament and submarine detection equipment, but these were still bare-bones protection against modern U-boats.

Worse, *Broadwater*'s wardroom, like all escort warships at that time, was thin on coordinated convoy tactics or antisubmarine battle plans. There was imperfect grasp of the U-boat pack system, or that German submarines often steamed on the surface at night, their low profiles making them difficult to spot. There was not yet a firmly established procedure to mentor *Broadwater*'s decision to drop behind the convoy in a brave but ill-considered attempt to trap a following U-boat. *U-101* heard and saw *Broadwater*'s approach long before firing its torpedo.

German submarine commanders called the months between June 1940 and June 1942 the "Happy Times." June 1942 was the worst month of the war for the Allies: U-boats sank 834,196 tons of shipping. In July convoy PQ-17 to Murmansk lost twenty-four of thirty-six ships to submarine and air attacks. U-boat luck was holding in September 1942, when RB-1's convoy of eight aging American-built river steamers departed the United States to become floating barracks, hospital ships, and cross-Channel packets for the eventual invasion of the Continent. None of them had ever sailed on any water but inland lakes and rivers. Volunteer British Merchant Navy men recruited in Liverpool provided the crews. An escort screen of four destroyers, including HMS *Veteran* (Lieutenant Commander Trevor Henry Garwood, RN) provided protection. A modern destroyer weighs more than 8,000 tons and is 500-plus feet long. *Veteran* displaced 1,325 tons, was 200 feet shorter and designed and armed with the Kaiser's fleet in mind. She was marginally qualified to perform in the war against Hitler. Nonetheless, optimism and good humor prevailed. Her commissioning captain was a determined personality with a wonderful sense of the absurd; on taking command, he immediately applied for Honorary Membership in the Company of Veteran Motorists. *Veteran*'s enigmatic motto was *Laudator temporis acti* or "Praise of times past." The company responded by making the ship a life member. A king-size Veteran Driver's Badge bearing the company's motto, "Care and Courtesy," was presented to the ship and affixed to the forward, center portion of the bridge.

Veteran took part in the Norwegian campaign in which Kansan Lieutenant Bill Taylor, RNVR, took to the air as a fighter pilot in the Fleet Air Arm. When New Yorker Surgeon Lieutenant Francis Hayes crossed *Veteran*'s quarterdeck for the first time he probably heard the crew buzz about the ship's partial credit for sinking *U-207* in the North Atlantic while escorting convoy SC-42. Also, King George VI had paid a personal visit aboard in Dover harbor. RB-1, known as the "Skimming Dish" convoy on account of their shallow draft, departed St. John's, Newfoundland, in the early afternoon of September 21, a few days after Hayes celebrated his thirtieth birthday. The little fleet was somewhat anachronistic even for the time. SS *Northland* was built in 1911. Her sister ship, SS *Southland*, was built in 1908. Adding to *Veteran*'s burden were scores of survivors rescued from the sea when *U-404* sank two of the steamers in mid-Atlantic.

After picking up forty-eight men from SS *Boston* (sunk on September 25 at 1637) and thirty men from SS *New York* (sunk at 2337 on the same day), *Veteran* had moved out sharply at sixteen knots to rejoin the remainder of the convoy. We can guess that Francis Hayes was busy at work. The dispensary and sick bay spaces on *Veteran* would have been a deck or two down, probably at about midships, in the most stable part of the vessel and with the least movement. Hayes and his hospital ratings were most likely tending to some of *Boston*'s and *New York*'s crew newly fished out of the ocean, some of the survivors in shock or injured. The torpedo struck *Veteran* on September 26, in position 55'00 North, 23'00 West. HMS *Vanoc* (Commander Charles Churchill, RN) reported losing contact soon after midnight at 0038. The surgeon and his helpers would have been totally absorbed by their tasks, unmindful of activities on the other side of the bulkhead. Even if *Veteran*'s munitions had not detonated, escape would have been difficult. To move litters of patients along a destroyer's narrow passageways is a precarious business at the best of times. To do so in total darkness or in the light of the dim blue glow of emergency blackout lights, with the regular crew racing in all directions, is all but impossible.

Loss of life was heavy: 78 rescued survivors and *Veteran*'s complement of 8 officers and 151 ratings—the entire ship's company—died in the attack.

SS *Yorktown*, in the same convoy, was lost along with eighteen of her crew at 2325, on September 26, to *U-619* (*Oberleutnant* Kurt Makowski), which was itself sunk with all hands nine days later. Lieutenant Derek Lee was a deck officer with the collateral job of security officer aboard HMS *Sardonyx*, another vintage destroyer brought out of the Royal Navy's fleet at the start of World War II. She picked up survivors from *Yorktown*. *Sardonyx* continued to scour the sea for further signs of human life. Lee censored as "Not for Publication" several photographs taken of the survivors as they climbed aboard his ship. *Sardonyx* vainly looked for others. A moment of hope was quickly disappointed as Verey lights were spotted in the autumn gloaming "when the light had almost gone and it was blowing a full gale with a heavy Atlantic swell." A couple of days later, Lee assisted with the rescue of three lifeboats filled with merchant seamen, their ship another torpedo casualty, who had "forced their nerve and sinew to cling onto this world for forty-eight hours," from the time their ship had been sent to the bottom. Lee got a mention in dispatches while serving on *Sardonyx* (National Archives, File ADM 199/1268, British Records Office).

The commander in chief, Western Approaches, ordered a search that continued until dusk on October 1. Of *Veteran*, nothing was ever recovered. After the war, captured German documents and the U-boat's commander shed more light on what had happened. Convoy RB-1 was attacked by a wolf pack consisting of *U-91*, *U-619*, and *U-404*. Over the period of September 25–26, 1942, Otto von Bülow had initially targeted the river steamers when *Veteran* unexpectedly hove into view. Shifting his priorities, he fired a torpedo spread at the destroyer and then dived to evade the counterattack. The U-boat's sonar reported two detonations. The total destruction of a ship, as was *Veteran*'s fate, is commonly due to the explosion of the magazine. The force of such a blast would account for the shocking suddenness of her complete disappearance and total absence of survivors.

Working that night at the Admiralty's top secret flag plot in London, Hayes' sister-in-law, Thea, on staff duty in the Women's Royal Naval Service (WRNS), was instructed to update the location of all naval ships. List in hand, she walked over to the map of the Atlantic and removed the cardboard identifier with the name HMS *Veteran*. Thea knew the implications of what she had done but tight secrecy stopped her from sharing the information with Hayes' wife, Georgette, who had to wait for the inevitable telegram with its terse, official phrasing, "The Admiralty deeply regrets to inform you." The adverb "deeply" was optional.

The death of *Veteran* did not play out on the news. There was no television; war details were tightly controlled. Security regulations in World War II censored all media as well as what sailors and soldiers wrote home from the battle lines. On both sides of the Atlantic, families crowded around radios concerned as much about the progress of the war itself as for their loved ones serving who knows where. Official reports of those who were injured, killed, or missing and presumed dead arrived by telegram. It was a time of secrecy. Hayes had just been home on leave in glowing health, playing tennis with his father on the family clay court, enjoying his small son, and dining in New York in dazzling full-dress naval uniform, when the telegram arrived in Middletown, New Jersey. Hayes' son was living there—without his mother—to escape the bombing in England. His grandparents had become his adoptive parents.

"What I remember most about childhood," wrote Hayes' niece,

> was the mystery of a deep sorrow that could not speak its name. Frankie was never talked about. Questions about him were not invited. Two photos of him (not to be remarked on) stood out prominently on Grandfather's dresser. Frank would never be one day older than these photographs. Yet he was always there somehow, with more of him waiting to be discovered in a locked-up cabinet or secret drawer. As children do, we made up stories to fill the vacuum: he was an heroic submarine commander going down in glory. He was alive, carrying secret messages to and from the Allies. Morse code that we learned and tried to implement could reach him.
>
> In short, he was both alive and dead. It is only now that I realize that Frank's parents, far from being secretive, were simply trying to move on.

> Lack of concrete information was also a reason for discretion. Records were unreliable until long after the war [and even today, such a scholarly institution as Gonville and Caius College, Cambridge, lists the death of Francis Mason Hayes on the wrong ship]. So Frankie, reported simply as "missing and presumed dead," was both alive and dead to the adults and us children as well. His mother believed that he was merely missing and in later years made an intense search to find him. (Ann Davenport Dixon [John Hayes' niece] correspondence to author, 20 October 2003, Charlotte Hammond papers)

The eight merchant ships of convoy RB-1 were SS *Boston*, Captain R. S. Young, Commodore; SS *New York*, Captain C. Mayers, Vice-Commodore; SS *Northland,* Captain James Beckett; SS *Southland*, Captain John Williams; SS *Yorktown*, Captain W. P. Boylan; SS *President Warfield*, Captain J. R. Williams; SS *New Bedford*, Captain R. Hardy; and rescue ship SS *Naushon*, Captain J. J. Murray.

President Warfield became a historic ship during the postwar years. In 1947 she was renamed *Exodus 1947*, the inspiration for the fictional ship *Exodus,* made famous by Leon Uris in his novel and in the popular film of the same name that followed. Rated for a maximum of 300 passengers and a crew of 69, the ship had 4,500 European Jewish refugees embarked in France for the ill-fated voyage to Haifa. A further historical curiosity is attached to *President Warfield*. The Old Bay Line steamer that plied the coastal route between Norfolk and Baltimore was named for the Baltimore Steam Packet Company's president, S. Davies Warfield, uncle of Wallis Warfield for whom Great Britain's King Edward VIII abdicated his throne.

The Atlantic war generated much bitterness. Venerable maritime traditions were often discarded, ordinary decency and mercy suppressed. Sailors from the defeated battleship *Bismarck* reached out for the safety of the heavy cruiser HMS *Dorsetshire*, ordered to pick up survivors. *Dorsetshire* steamed slowly among heads bobbing in the swell and tossed ropes over the side for the men in the water to grab and climb aboard. British seamen assisted about 90 Germans to safety and the destroyer HMS *Maori* had fished out another 25 survivors when *Dorsetshire* got under way. *Maori* followed. Hundreds of swimming men, some badly wounded, were abandoned. Of more than 2,200 sailors, fewer than 120 were rescued. *Vae victis.* A year later the Japanese sank *Dorsetshire* with several direct hits leading to the detonation of her magazine; she sank in minutes. The U.S. Navy rescued most of her complement of 600.

In contrast to the fate that befell *Bismarck*'s sailors, Lieutenant Bill Homans did a remarkable thing. He jumped from his British warship into the Irish Sea and swam toward a downed Luftwaffe aircraft to save the pilot from drowning. Homans recalled that his fellow Royal Navy officers were not pleased with him. We can guess that the lack of enthusiasm was due to the disparities between their relative proximity to the war at that time. British families were daily under threat of being obliterated by German bombs. British cities and homes were routine targets for destruction. The idealistic young American's native country was neutral; his home was perfectly safe. The Luftwaffe could not menace his family in any way. Homans had not learned to hate.

The third volunteer of "The First Three" at the Royal Naval College, Charles Porter, crossed the Atlantic aboard HMS *Repulse*, a battle cruiser that, a month earlier, had taken part in the pursuit of *Bismarck*. Not much later, *Repulse* suffered the same fate as HMS *Dorsetshire*, sunk in the Far East by the Japanese. Porter's orders put him as assistant operations officer on the staff of the commander in chief, the Nore, at Chatham. As it had been for a hundred years, the Nore Command, near the entrance of the River Thames, was a major operational headquarters directing coastal shipping routes to the commercial harbors of London and up the east coast of England; the headquarters was housed eighty feet belowground in a bunker.

A formerly indifferent student, dedicated sailor, and career real estate agent in New England, Porter now became aware of what was going on in the Royal Navy at the highest levels and also what was being planned. The Nore later became important as a staging area for Allied armies in northwestern Europe after the Normandy invasion in 1944, an epic event in which Porter was destined to participate.

Henry Ripley joined the largest single group of American volunteers assembled at Greenwich during the war. His contemporaries at the college were Alex Cherry, David Gibson, Edmund Kittredge, Carl "Leaping Dane" Konow, and George Hoague. They all completed their training on the day following Japan's attack on the U.S. Pacific Fleet at Pearl Harbor, Hawaii. Hickam Field was still billowing smoke when Hoague reported to HMS *Ausonia,* a 19,000-

ton armed merchant cruiser, where he served as a deck officer alongside Carl Konow. Ripley served on Canadian corvettes assigned to the North Atlantic. Monsarrat's *Three Corvettes* gives a glimpse of what life was like aboard one of these small ships in Atlantic waters. "Our wardroom consisted, apart from a superb professional in the captain," wrote Monsarrat, "of one Australian motor-car salesman, one gas-company cashier, one barrister and . . . a holiday sailor, a free-lance writing hack with his shirt tails hanging out of his trousers." They sailed "over ground literally strewn with dead sailors, blown up, burned to death, shredded by the sea, sucked down, *drowned*—the most awful word in a sailor's word book . . . the sea now seemed poisoned for ever."

Californian John Leggat got his training at HMS *Drake* before reporting to HMS *Woolston* (motto: "Where Our Forefathers Lead We Follow"), an escort destroyer of the V&W class, so called because their individual names all began with one or the other letter. *Woolston* was under command of the Nore and detached for defense of Atlantic convoys in the Western Approaches. Commander W. J. Phipps, OBE, was *Woolston*'s skipper just prior to Leggat's time aboard. Phipps' diary is an intimate glimpse into the grueling wartime shipboard routine that Leggat experienced. First was the wildly variable weather: "Blowing up again," "Raining very hard and thoroughly beastly outlook," "Blinding rain and hail," "Visibility practically nil." There was the poor discipline of the convoys *Woolston* was sent to protect; Merchant Navy captains could not be depended on to reliably share in Navy discipline or take Navy orders. "[The] convoy would be stupid and went the wrong side," was one of many similar comments Phipps entered in his log. The Admiralty further added to *Woolston*'s burden with over-demands and occasionally conflicting orders that did not account for rapidly changing conditions.

Then there were the Germans. Heinkels, Junker 88s, and Dorniers dropped their bombs and strafed the ships. Sea mines trapped the unwary and the unlucky. When mines were spotted, *Woolston*'s marksmen used rifle fire to pierce the steel shells, sending the mine to the bottom, waterlogged. Probable U-boats were attacked, not always successfully but also not without resourcefulness: "First attacked a good target," Phipps wrote, "but can't have been anything. Got lots of fish and went alongside them and picked them up." E-boats came with shocking suddenness, with no warning, under cover of a smoke screen, and with devastating effect launched their torpedoes: "Suddenly astern there was the most terrific blaze up and it looked at first like a tanker on fire. Two great balls of fire went up and the whole sea for about half a mile looked to be a roaring inferno."

This part of the war went on day and night, without respite. Phipps wrote and Leggatt found out, "No rest. No rest."

In April 1942 Leggat went to HMS *King Alfred* at Hove (familiar to some of the other volunteers) for more schooling and then spent eight months at sea with HM *LST 301*. There were never enough LSTs in the whole war. "All turned upon LSTs," wrote Winston Churchill in his book *Closing the Ring*. In May 1943 Leggat reported aboard HMS *Richmond*, a former American World War I "four-piper." *Richmond* protected the convoy lifelines across the Atlantic all the way to the Arctic Ocean to Russia. War in Arctic waters was especially arduous because there were two relentless foes: the Germans and the bitter weather. Both enemies pushed men to the limits of endurance. About 1,400 merchant ships in seventy-eight convoys threaded their way past German air and sea defenses to supply the Russian army. More than 100 Allied merchant ships and warships were lost.

Virginia gentleman and midwestern financier, Kittredge went on a short naval gunnery course at Chatham before reporting aboard the light cruiser HMS *Diomede* deployed in the South Atlantic. His military experience quickly broadened when he was reassigned to a commando unit.

Alex Cherry got a fiery introduction to life afloat. At the end of his four months' training, he asked to use his seven days' graduation leave aboard a destroyer on active service. He got his wish and was assigned to HMS *Winchester* (another of the V&W class) in the dangerous waters of the North Sea, off England's east coast. The area became "Bomber Alley" by day and "E-boat Alley" at night. (The German S-boot [*schnell* translates as fast] became an E-boat in the Royal Navy's lexicon.) Aboard a warship in the thick of things, Cherry was impressed by his first engagement with the enemy. He wrote about "wary destroyers guarding the rear positions, already occupied with attacking aircraft, suddenly espied shadows on the surface, streaking towards the convoy. Enemy E-boats! Like a swarm of bees they came on." His baptism of fire came from Luftwaffe Dornier bombers in a direct attack on his ship (on him personally, he felt at the time) (*Yankee RN*, London: Jarrolds, 1951).

Cherry went on to serve aboard HMS *Reading* on Newfoundland convoy defense in the Western Atlantic. There he developed his "Proposal to Improve the Present Convoy System." What he worked out in detail was the shift to a single line abreast formation with a distance of five cables between ships armed with ASDIC and depth charge throwers, and operated by small contingents of U.S. and RN officers and ratings. It was an aggressive, thoughtful plan that was not adopted probably because of shortages in personnel and weaponry as well as the rapid ascendancy of other effective counter–U-boat equipment and tactics, like radar and the growing umbrella of air cover. Cherry went on to serve on HMS *Evadne*, a yacht converted to a submarine chaser, on the sloop HMS *Wren* as first lieutenant assigned to the English Channel operating area, and on HMS *Riou*. *Wren*, *Starling,* and the frigates *Loch Killin*, *Loch Fada*, *Lochy,* and *Dominica* were part of the famous Second Escort Group, commanded by Captain F. J. Walker, CB, DSO and three bars. Walker's traditions continued after his death; the group went into battle with its signature tune, "A-Hunting We Will Go." On one occasion, *Wren* engaged a surfaced U-boat with its 4-inch Oerlikon guns; the U-boat (*U-473*) sank in five minutes. It was Cherry's gun position that took out the submarine and he helped to interrogate the survivors.

After this incident, a journalist wrote, "Lieut. Commander Cherry, *Wren*'s No. 1, who is an American and a former New York banker, said, 'It is obvious that the morale of the younger Germans is sinking. As prisoners they are very disappointed and seem to express the hope that Hitler will pull another trick out of the bag' " ("They Killed U-Boats in English Channel," *Evening Express*, 23 September 1944). Cherry was rightfully proud of his service under Walker's command. Walker was the only man named in a list prepared by the Admiralty of the Navy's greatest wartime achievements. He died of exhaustion, worn out by his dedicated pursuit of the enemy.

When Cherry became first lieutenant on HMS *Braithwaite* fitting out in Boston, Massachusetts, there was an incident that former crew members recall to this day. Following several other crises, Cherry discovered that the ship's silverware had been sold by the disgruntled crew to a local restaurant for the price of a good night's drinking ashore. Next day, *Braithwaite*'s skipper temporarily absent, Cherry assembled the crew for a no-holds-barred haranguing. Veterans of the moment remember language spiced with "thieving scum" and "unfit for the honor of serving under the White Ensign." At the conclusion of his delivery Cherry ordered the men to stand down for their customary morning break. To a man, they all stayed rooted in place and refused to return to work.

Cherry considered asking a nearby British cruiser to send over a troop of Royal Marines with bayonets fixed to arrest the mutinous complement. Further escalation was avoided when *Braithwaite*'s captain returned aboard. A bureaucratic deus ex machina saved Cherry from any investigative unpleasantness. His appointment arrived at that moment promoting him to lieutenant commander. He was now too senior for the job on *Braithwaite*. After being aboard for two weeks, he was transferred. HMS *Braithwaite* went on to earn battle honors for her participation at Normandy on D-day.

Alex Cherry's seagoing career received good marks in navigation, antisubmarine warfare, and, most especially, for his staff officer work. In the annual evaluation of his subordinate's quality of service, HMS *Evadne*'s commanding officer wrote that Cherry "is continually in demand by all grades of USN officers for assistance and cooperation and at one period was lent to a flotilla of U.S. fleet destroyers" (Cherry correspondence, Michael Sabatell collection). As one of the ship's officers who daily interact with other ranks there were problems. Early praise for leadership took a precipitous downward turn as *Evadne*'s deployment lengthened. By the end of the six-month evaluation period something had gone badly wrong. Cherry's marks plummeted and he was transferred. While others aboard HMS *Wren* received decorations for the U-boat that was actually sunk by Cherry's gun, Cherry himself was ignored. He felt the slight was due to the captain's dislike of Americans. Years after the war, Cherry was still chasing the recognition that he felt had been wrongfully denied him but he never lost his affection for the Royal Navy.

The Royal Navy had made David Gibson a destroyer sailor. He excelled as a seaman and later, at the end of the war, got three commands of his own. Following gunnery training at Chatham, he was ordered to HMS *Burnham* (ex–USS *Aulick*), part of the Newfoundland Escort Force, based at St. Johns. *Burnham* "escorted convoys of between fifty and ninety ships to and from Britain from St. John's to Londonderry, Northern Ireland," Gibson told his son. "My duties were deck and anti-submarine warfare officer, supervising the sonar and radar personnel's continuous sweep searches for enemy submarines. It was a wonderful ship with a wonderful crew," he said (correspondence, winter 2000, Eric Gibson collection). After the war the crew formed a club and met at annual reunions.

Gibson vividly remembered, "If a tanker or a munitions carrier was fatally torpedoed it became a fireball and survivors, if any, were few and when fished from the sea were coated with fuel oil from the ship's ruptured bunkers, and boiler and engine room personnel badly scalded from fractured steam lines. Many died rapidly from the ingestion of fuel oil or invalided for life with debilitating lung complications. Vessels with heavy cargo such as armored vehicles and industrial equipment sank rapidly." Maintaining convoy discipline was crucial; "those ships which escaped the enemy's attack *never* altered course or speed except to avoid overrunning a casualty ship and then returned to its station from the next undamaged ship ahead." Gibson served with *Burnham* until the end of 1943 when the ship was "certified as no longer fit for convoy duty" (ibid.).

In the 1952 film *Glory at Sea* (originally titled *The Gift Horse*) Trevor Howard is the captain of one of the fifty tired and overage destroyers on Lend-Lease to England by the United States, just like HMS *Burnham* and the other ex-USN warships to which the volunteers were assigned. Alex Cherry complained that some of the episodes in *Glory at Sea* were lifted wholesale from his book and threatened legal action. The film's story centers on professional and amateur sailors like Gibson who kept these ships in service despite multiple breakdowns and inexperienced officers, and the relentless challenges thrown at them by the enemy and the sea. The crew included a Canadian first officer and an American citizen (played by Sonny Tufts, a Yale graduate) who chose to enlist in the Royal Navy. The film is a first-rate dramatization of heroic performance during the Battle of the Atlantic that is substantiated by England's wartime history.

Gibson was promoted to lieutenant and took his seabag to HMS *Tyler* (ex–USS *Buckley*), a destroyer escort. Roy Emmington, a rating aboard *Tyler*, remembered the routine. "Thirty days at sea looking after Atlantic convoys then seven days in port for boiler cleans" ("Another Job for an Ex-Ganges Boy," NavSource.org). Gibson is one of the few volunteers who did not shift over to the U.S. Navy. He stayed with the British to the end, despite the poor pay and meager rations. His greatest adventure was yet to come: the invasion of Europe.

Ed Russell served as a deck officer on the heavy cruiser HMS *Norfolk*, deployed out of Scapa Flow for convoy work in Atlantic and Arctic waters. He, too, was fated to participate at the Normandy landings.

Harry Howlett, a rating aboard HMML *115* remembered Oswald Deiter as "a great skipper. In fact, we used to call him the 'mad skipper,' but the risks he took were calculated. The crew got used to it after a while" (correspondence, 5 August 2001, authors' collection). He also remembered Deiter's early morning swims in the icy waters of Loch Lyne, and especially one occasion when Deiter had to be rescued after getting severe cramps. Oswald Deiter was the most unlikely sailor among the volunteers. Uniforms, salutes, "shun! Lefright! lefright! lefright! Lock and load! Fire at will!" and the rest of it had never entered his vocabulary. He was portly in stature and sedentary by vocation. His medical success had made him relatively famous and financially secure and he lived comfortably with his wife, Ellaline, in one of London's most exclusive areas. He was also much too old for war in any theater. There was nothing whatever in his background to signal military excellence, but looks can deceive; Deiter excelled as a naval officer.

The Royal Navy does not lightly give command of its warships to foreigners, no matter what the tonnage, but Deiter was selected. Following antisubmarine training at HMS *Nimrod* and HMS *Seahawk*, both shore stations in Culdrose, Scotland, Deiter was appointed skipper of HMML *115*, a Fairmile shallow-draft vessel armed chiefly with rapid-fire weapons and depth charges. The boat had a crew of fifteen and was used for coastal patrol, hunting U-boats and E-boats, and defending against the occasional marauding Luftwaffe aircraft. HMML *115* was based in the tiny port of Ardrishaig at the north end of Loch Lyne, and she also assisted with the training of miniature submarine crews.

During one of war's lighter moments Deiter was sent on a courtesy and goodwill visit to Canvey Island, Essex. The town had adopted his boat and so on Friday, June 18, 1943, wanted to cap the affiliation with an exchange of plaques at the local council offices. The ceremony was followed by a parade in which the whole crew participated. A visiting dignitary thanked the people of the island for "supporting that sea-power on which, from the days of Elizabeth, the safety, honor and welfare of the country had chiefly depended." Lieutenant Dieter was loudly cheered (Janet Penn, "Warship Week 1942: The Week Canvey Pulled out All the Stops," Canvey Community Archives).

Like Deiter, George Hoague went to antisubmarine duties. He left Greenwich and then completed a short naval gunnery course at Chatham before reporting to the sloop HMS *Sennen*, where one of his wardroom companions was fellow American volunteer Ed Ferris. *Sennen* ploughed the waters between Gibraltar and Freetown. Hoague transferred to the U.S. Navy in late autumn 1942, retaining the rank of lieutenant. Not all the volunteers who transferred kept their Royal Navy seniority. In Hoague's case, the Royal Navy had given him a watch-keeping certificate; in other words, he had deck officer qualifications identical to those of a regular Royal Navy officer of the same rank. The U.S. Navy got a fully trained, credentialed officer—and, as we shall see, a man who pulled his weight during Operation Overlord, the invasion of Normandy.

In the prewar years France occupied a warm spot in the hearts of Americans. American schoolboys looked to the World War I Lafayette Escadrille for inspiration. Had France gone to war at the time of the Munich crisis, Americans would have flocked to her defense. Alex Cherry wrote, "As for Great Britain, most of us felt we had nothing in common." After Munich, France was gone and England was engaged in a war for which it was woefully ill-prepared. All that "remained was to help the nation that still fought for freedom," Cherry had vowed (*Yankee RN*). Some vocal Americans energetically opposed U.S. participation in another European conflict.

As Hitler bolstered his forces, Joseph Kennedy—FDR's envoy to Britain—energetically spread an isolationist point of view. Congress enacted the Neutrality Act. Many Americans predicted England had no fight left in her and would capitulate. "Hitler will be in Buckingham Palace in two weeks," announced Kennedy in London as France fell. Ever mindful of his own self-interest, Kennedy used his ambassadorial clout to ship home 200,000 cases of Haig & Haig Scotch lest the Wehrmacht deny him the opportunity. Cherry feared that England would give up even as he was at sea, a newly commissioned RN volunteer. It was a perilous hour. "All that was decent in life hung by a thread." Hitler's inexorable march notwithstanding, just like the people with whom they had made common cause, the American volunteers were undaunted. They considered themselves fortunate to have been accepted in the RNVR. Gibson could have spoken for them all when he said, "I was a very lucky fellow!" (correspondence, Eric Gibson collection).

5 The Air War

When Hitler had conquered most of the European continent he was ready to engorge England. Operation Sea Lion was the planned amphibious invasion of Great Britain. Before preparations for landings could be advanced, the Luftwaffe sought to win control of the air by attacking Royal Air Force fields, radar stations, and other installations. Once the Luftwaffe had control of the air the theory was that it could compensate for the weakness of the Kriegsmarine and defeat the Royal Navy.

By July 4, 1940, the situation was so grim that Churchill felt it was necessary to send a letter addressed to "All persons holding responsible positions in the Government, the Fighting services or in the Civil Departments." It was "their duty," he cautioned, "to maintain a spirit of alert and confident energy." He sternly added, "The Prime Minister expects all His Majesty's servants in high places to set an example of steadiness and resolution. They should check and rebuke expressions of loose and ill-digested opinion in their circles, or by their subordinates. They should not hesitate to report, or if necessary remove, any officers or officials who are found to be consciously expressing a disturbing or depressing influence, and whose talk is calculated to spread alarm and despondency." Commanding officers of ships and squadrons were included in the addressee list (Lieutenant Commander W. J. Phipps journal aboard HMS *Woolston*, October 1939–April 1941, Imperial War Museum Documents 75/105/1).

This phase of the war evolved into the Battle of Britain and lasted from July 10 to October 31, 1940. It ended with the defeat of the German effort.

After the war, Soviet interrogators asked Field Marshal Gerd von Rundstedt, Germany's preeminent military commander, which battle he thought was the most decisive of the war, expecting him to say Stalingrad. The field marshal answered, "the Battle of Britain" (Stephen Bungav, *The Most Dangerous Enemy*, London: Aurum Press, 2000). Describing Battle of Britain pilots and what they had accomplished, Winston Churchill famously said in a radio broadcast to the nation, "Never in the field of human conflict was so much owed by so many to so few" (BBC broadcast, 20 August 1940).

The Battle of Britain was followed by the Blitz, the massive bombing campaign against major cities and ports. London alone was targeted and bombed for fifty-seven consecutive nights. More than 20,000 people were killed and 1.4 million were made homeless.

The Cavendish on Jermyn Street was badly damaged by a bomb and seventy-eight-year-old Rosa Lewis was injured. She went on unperturbed. Walton Hannah, the curate at her church across the street, St. James' Piccadilly, remembered how undaunted Rosa was. "She taxied off to a hotel for a few days, shouting at [the] poor long-suffering man-of-all-work: 'Everything has got to be put back as it was by the end of the week. *Everything*: d'you understand?' " (Harrison, *Rosa*). To help raise the curate's morale after St. James' was bombed (this was part of the campaign to attack historic landmarks, nicknamed "Baedecker raids," after the famous holiday guidebook), Rosa opened a bottle of 1911 Bollinger, a wonderfully rare vintage. Air raids continued for the duration of the war, ending with the desperate finale when V-1 "Doodlebugs" (nickname for German *Vergeltungswaffe*) and V-2 rockets landed indiscriminately, and with devastating impact, throughout London and its environs.

Before he entered the Royal Navy, Francis Hayes was a surgeon on full-time emergency duty at Greenwich's Miller General Hospital. Greenwich took a fearful beating throughout the war, especially at the outset when the destruction was especially fierce and protracted.

One eyewitness was the Canadian conductor and professor Brock McElheran, who described a typical scene of the devastation following an air raid: "One woman was directing the firemen and giving particulars of the residents to a policeman and an air raid warden. She was about 35, of moderate build, and was wearing a dark red dress now whitened with dust. Her face was completely black with soot [and] when she talked her teeth gleamed white.

A trickle of sticky blood oozed from a cut over one eyebrow. The blood, too, was darkened by the soot. Her manner was calm, capable, and friendly. As she pointed to one wrecked house I heard her say, 'Then there's old Mrs. Jackson in Number 16B—that's that one,' as if she were directing a new postman." McElheran continued, "Two firemen were looking around the wall at something I couldn't see. A third stepped over towards me and shouted, 'For God's sake, somebody get an ambulance. There's a woman in 'ere with 'er guts 'anging out' " (Brock McElheran, *V-Bombs and Weathermaps*, Quebec: McGill-Queen's University Press, 1995).

A naval officer assigned to London, Commander Alfred Stanford, USNR, was an eyewitness. He wrote,

> People, men, women and children of London, knew the war not as something they read about, but as a wild beast that turned on them every day. Perhaps because they had no houses, perhaps for human company and a cup of tea when the raid was on, thousands nightly still crawled into the slatted bunks that lined the Underground stations. Every man, woman and child knew what followed the rising and falling wail of the sirens. That undulating sound penetrated through every habitation in the darkened city with chilling dread. The sound of planes was not far behind. Then the distant crump of a bomb on its mark would punctuate the stillness of the waiting city. Marker flares burned brightly overhead and the drone of planes from the clouds increased as the main flight came in. (Alfred Stanford, *Force Mulberry*)

He continued,

> The people knew what the whistling sound of a nearby bomb was like. They knew the blinding orange flash that followed as a block of houses was ripped apart. Their ears knew well the roar that followed and rose like a wall of solid sound against the sharp cracks of the AA guns; then with the rolling thunder of toppling masonry finally dropped into silence. The choking dust of centuries of living filled the air, the lungs, the clothing. The dust of old plaster, the dust between the floors, the dust under stairs all suddenly vomited up into the whole sky, penetrated everywhere, with perhaps an occasional crash of a single pane of glass falling into the street

> or the cries of the warden directing the first search party into the heaped-up ruin. (ibid.)

Londoner Dobbie Dobinson said,

> The raids continued each night and the East End of London suffered terribly. My turn finally came when they dropped four landmines by parachute. The first of their kind. I was told that a lot of people, such as air raid wardens and police, were killed unnecessarily as they rushed towards the parachutes, thinking they were German airmen landing. When the mines exploded, the blast took everything above ground level. People were just blown to pieces and trees in the garden were stripped of leaves and branches; many bodies, or parts of them, were resting in any remaining trees. ("Lord Haw Haw and the Blackshirts," BBC, *WW2 People's War,* 29 July 2003)

In spite of the fatigue and terror there was an exhilaration in the people, a spirit of obstinate good humor no matter what.

John Winant tells a story in his autobiography "of a woman in Bath who was brought in to a Rest Centre after a raid. She had a black eye and was bruised and shaken. . . . She was asked the usual questions, among them whether she was married and, if so, whether her husband was alive. When she replied in the affirmative they said, 'Where is your husband?' She looked up at once and said, 'In Libya, the bloody coward!' " [Her husband was battling Rommel's *Afrika Korps* in Libya.] (*A Letter from London,* London: Hodder and Stoughton, 1947).

To protect old Mrs. Jackson, Dobbie Dobinson, the Rest Centre woman, and all their neighbors throughout the country, there were about two thousand very young men in their Royal Air Force Spitfire and Hurricane fighter aircraft who dueled with the Luftwaffe a mile and more above the countryside. Seven Americans serving with the Royal Air Force participated in the Battle of Britain, pilot officers all (second lieutenant): Art Donahue, DFC; William Fiske (cited below); John Haviland, DFC; Vernon "Shorty" Keough (killed February 15, 1941); Phillip Leckrone (killed January 5, 1941); Andrew Mamedoff (killed May 8, 1941); and Eugene "Red" Tobin (killed September 2, 1941).

In Grosvenor Square in London, the new U.S. ambassador was as overtly upbeat and pro-British as his predecessor had been cynical and defeatist. John Winant was a remarkable personality in his own right and a perfect fit for the job following the anti-British performance of the man he replaced, Joseph Kennedy—a future president's father. For a better-informed point of view and a personality more suited to the times, Roosevelt, a Democrat, had turned to the former Republican governor of New Hampshire, Winant, who stayed at his post throughout the war, Blitz included.

Volunteer fighter pilots were the largest American group in British forces, and they liked their ambassador. The men of the Eagle Squadron invited Winant to be their guest of honor on the first Thanksgiving he spent in England.

The same Colonel Sweeney who had organized Americans for the Home Guard also recruited them for the Royal Air Force. Some 240 pilots and ground support personnel, enough for three fighter squadrons, fought in the air battles over Britain and wore the U.S. Eagle tab on the shoulder of their uniform. Sweeney was the squadron's first (honorary, non-flying, and non-operational) commanding officer. The men were not salted among regular Royal Air Force units because the publicity value of a group of Yanks in British uniform was priceless, but also because Americans had a reputation for spirited independence leading to disorderliness. Among the pilots were barnstormers, crop dusters, stunt fliers, and sportsmen. The youngest was Gregory "Gus" Daymond, nineteen, of California, who once piloted an ice-cream mogul. The oldest was Paul Joseph Haaren, forty-eight, also of California, a movie flier.

The mix included a classic American immigrant success story. Newspapers covered the naturalization of a Greek immigrant who had used all his money in the United States to buy flying lessons. "When I was in the States I had very happy days. Today is the most happiest day in my life when I am an American citizen," said a cheerful Army Air Corps fighter pilot, Lieutenant Spiros "Steve" Pissanos at the ceremony that made him a U.S. citizen (www.fourthfightergroup.com/resource/pisanosprofile).

Pissanos left his native Greece in 1938, landed in New York with eight dollars in his pocket, got a thirteen-dollar-a-week job in a bakery and within two months saved enough to start flying lessons. He joined the Eagle Squadron in 1941 and then transferred to U.S. Fighter Command where he became an ace in the 8th Air Force, with seven victories to his credit.

Sweeney's nephew, Robert Sweeney, also joined. He garnered the most personal media attention because he had won the British amateur golf championship in 1937 and was a steady companion of socialite Barbara Hutton.

Some of the American pilots had extraordinary careers in the Royal Air Force. Wing commander Guy Gibson, VC, DSO and bar, DFC and bar, persuaded Long Island, New York–born J. C. McCarthy, DSO, DFC and bar, to join the famous Dam Busters. Squadron leader "Arizona Wildcat" Lance C. Wade, DSO, DFC and two bars, became the highest-scoring American-born ace in the Royal Air Force, with twenty-five victories. Yale University graduate John Gillespie Magee Jr. flew Spitfires in the Battle of Britain and was killed in a midair collision on December 11, 1941. Flying among cumulus clouds one bright day he quickly wrote a poem afterward (Linda Granfield, *High Flight: A Story of World War II*, Toronto: Tundra Books, 1999). "High Flight" (which survives because Magee mailed a copy to his parents) became a hymn of exultation for all who pilot fixed-wing aircraft:

High Flight
Oh, I have slipped the surly bonds of earth
And danced the skies on laughter-silvered wings;
Sunward I've climbed, and joined the tumbling mirth
Of sun-split clouds—and done a hundred things
You have not dreamed of

The first U.S. citizen to be killed in the Battle of Britain over the quilted hedgerows of England's "green and pleasant land" is remembered in the crypt of St. Paul's Cathedral, London. Among monuments raised to honor some of the most illustrious of Britain's sons was

Pilot Officer
William Meade Lindsley Fiske III
Royal Air Force
An American Citizen
Who Died
That England Might Live
August 18th 1940

John Winant unveiled the plaque. The British Secretary of State for Air captured the spirit of all the volunteers of whatever shade of uniform when he said, "Here was a young man [Fiske was twenty-nine years old at the time of his death] for whom life held much. Under no kind of compulsion he came to fight for Britain. He came and he fought, and he died" (Pilot Officer W. M. L. "Billy" Fiske, 601 Squadron RAFVR, www.fiskes.co.uk). The hymn they sang that day was made famous in the American Civil War, "The Battle Hymn of the Republic."

Like his compatriots serving in the Royal Navy, Fiske came from a privileged background. He won a gold medal in the five-man bobsled contest at the 1928 Winter Olympics and another in the four-man contest at the 1932 Winter Games; he remains the youngest Olympic bobsled gold medalist in the history of the sport. And like some of the RNVR volunteers who also visited Hitler's Germany in the 1930s, Fiske was appalled by what he saw. He was so taken aback that he declined to participate in the February 1936 Winter Olympics held in Garmisch-Partenkirchen in Bavaria.

As rich and celebrated as Fiske was, obtaining the authority to wear a British uniform did not come as easily to him as it did to Draper Kauffman or Bill Taylor who got their interview and naval commissions quickly. Tugging at every available social string, Fiske was able to wangle an appointment with a high-ranking Royal Air Force officer and prepared for the interview by playing a round of golf to get "that healthy look." Adding, "Needless to say, for once, I had a quiet Saturday night. I didn't want to have eyes looking like blood-stained oysters the next day" (ibid.).

Billy Fiske met his fate at the controls of his Hurricane, engaging a patrol of Stuka dive-bombers 12,000 feet above the county of Sussex. His remains rest in the southeast corner of Boxgrove Cemetery not far from where his body was recovered. On either side of his grave lie British soldiers, a sapper in the Royal Engineers and a corporal in the East Lancashire Regiment. Fiske's grave displays a small Stars and Stripes. Lord Brabazon of Tara said of him, "We thank America for sending us the perfect sportsman" (Granfield, *High Flight*).

The Eagle Squadron's first commanding officer was the thirty-five-year-old erstwhile USN aviator, USMC pilot, and RNVR Fleet Air Arm lieutenant, William Taylor.

After he joined the Royal Navy in September 1939, Taylor went to fighter school. He flew Gloster Gladiators over the North Sea, staging in Scotland and the Orkney Isles where the main mission was to guard the British fleet assembled at their base in Scapa Flow. In April 1940 his squadron joined the carrier HMS *Glorious* flying sorties in support of British army landings in Norway. Taylor's first combat was against a Heinkel bomber. He was next posted to the carrier HMS *Furious* serving with the Home Fleet in the Atlantic and then to the carrier HMS *Argus,* in Force H. Force H was established in June 1940, in the aftermath of the sinking of French naval assets at Mers-el-Kébir, to compensate for the absence of the French navy in the Western Mediterranean.

Soon after Taylor's reassignment, *Glorious* returned from Norway escorted by two destroyers, HMS *Ardent* and HMS *Acasta.* The group was surprised by the battle cruisers *Scharnhorst* and *Gneisenau.* The Germans engaged at fourteen miles with accurate gunfire, sinking the carrier. *Acasta* was the last to go under, ninety-eight minutes after the action began but not before firing her torpedoes, one of which struck *Scharnhorst.* That day, 1,500 men perished. A Norwegian merchant ship picked up some of the 46 survivors from *Glorious* and transferred them to HMS *Veteran,* which signaled the first news of the loss of the carrier and her escort ships to the commander in chief, Home Fleet.

Taylor observed the Royal Navy with intelligence and keen attention to tactical and scientific details. At sea he noted that increased squadron successes in air combat interceptions against enemy bombers was due to a combination of forward projection by meeting the enemy as far as possible from home territory, and the extended sunlight offered by the extreme northern latitude. Long summer days and nighttime half-light vastly extended visibility over the North Sea and along the enemy-occupied Norwegian coast.

He also learned about "fighter direction" which guided fighter aircraft already in the air and coordinated their operations. Taylor recalled, "We were able to keep all of the German bombers from closing in on our fleet. No ship was bombed or even did we have a near miss during that period. However, our aircraft were not fast enough to chase the German bombers which turned away and jettisoned their bombs before we had a chance to intercept them" (William B. G. Taylor, 1905–1991 scrapbook collection, Garber Facility, National Air & Space Museum, Smithsonian Institution, Suitland, Maryland).

The great secret to fighter direction control was an interlocking chain of radar stations that linked Great Britain from one end to the other—from John O'Groats to Land's End—stretching the horizon exponentially. By carefully noting the ship's antenna array Taylor guessed that the same type of detection equipment, radar, was employed on British warships. The Luftwaffe failed to grasp the implications of this critical, evolving electronic warfare capability until it was much too late.

Taylor reported that the Royal Navy embarked few aircraft and operated them more in single units than as a large fighting force, as the Americans did. He described the Fleet Air Arm as desperately in need of pilots and aircraft. Despite the appalling lack of resources they did an excellent job, he said. He attributed their success to the direction and control system. Without it, he believed that, with its comparatively few aircraft, the Royal Navy would never have been able to intercept more than a fraction of the attacking bombers. Taylor did everything he could to amass information on how this tight control was accomplished, and he made periodic reports of his findings to the U.S. air attaché in London.

While the United States gathered scientific intelligence, the British government looked for ways to exploit the public relations appeal of the American volunteers to promote Britain's cause in the United States. Late in 1940 the Royal Navy sent Taylor home to lobby for more fighter aircraft and, especially, pilots. By the time he arrived back in the United States, France had fallen. This sudden change in the situation made available four different types of military aircraft due to the cancellation of French government contracts. Taylor succeeded in getting one hundred of the stubby new Grumman F4F "Wildcat" fighters, but finding qualified flying personnel was much more difficult. The chief of the Bureau of Aeronautics, Rear Admiral Jack Towers, told Taylor all available pilots were being diverted to Chennault's Flying Tigers.

The F4Fs were factory delivered at the rate of five planes per week. In mid-July Taylor reported to the Admiralty that the planes could be flown from the Grumman factory in Bethpage, Long Island, entirely ready for active service. He reckoned that by the middle of August, twenty of the planes could be brought into service and suggested that Fleet Air Arm pilots should be sent over "in mufti" to ferry the planes to a waiting British carrier. Adding to the F4F trove, Taylor also found fifty available Vought-Sikorsky V-156 "Vindicator" dive-bombers. Guns, gun sights, and radios had not been found but he believed that the missing equipment could be quickly located. He also advised that changes were required to the planes to make them better suited for Royal Navy carrier operations. The modifications were adopted and the aircraft was re-designated as the V-156B1 and given the name Chesapeake. Taylor helped convert the fighters to British shipboard use and arranged for delivery to Britain, where he worked for a month getting the aircraft reassembled and allocated to fighter squadrons.

While in the United States, Taylor met with the ubiquitous Charles Sweeney who sold him on the notion that he would make an ideal commanding officer of the all-American Eagle Squadron (No. 71 Squadron) being formed at that moment. Taylor agreed to the switch and, accordingly, the Royal Navy was asked to release him. On October 3, 1940, the Air Ministry commissioned Taylor into the Royal Air Force Volunteer Reserve. The transfer ceremony was made in front of newsreel cameras and a large press contingent; Taylor looked shy and oddly out of place. Afterward a private, cool meeting was held with a somewhat dyspeptic Air Vice Marshal Trafford Leigh-Mallory who had opposed the establishment of a squadron of Americans in the first place. In his First World War experience Leigh-Mallory had found Americans to be totally undisciplined.

In a brand-new uniform, Squadron Leader (lieutenant commander, or major) Taylor arrived at RAF Church Fenton, only to be dismayed to find that Squadron Leader Walter Churchill had preceded him as the commanding officer. Unwilling to be a mere figurehead, Taylor made his objections to Fighter Command and was ordered, at his request, to 242 Squadron while the dual commanding officer issue was sorted out. Thus Taylor gained valuable operational experience in an active fighter squadron under the direction of Douglas Bader (later, Group Captain Sir Douglas Bader, CBE, DSO and bar, DFC and bar). Bader's exploits as an air ace following the loss of both legs in a prewar plane crash, and as a troublesome and irritating POW, were dramatized in the film *Reach for the Sky*.

During the months with the Squadron, Taylor joined in interceptions against German aircraft, flying wing for Bader, but for the most part he spent his time in the dry business of learning tactics and the structure of Royal Air Force organizations. He still wanted what had been promised: command of

71 Squadron. And he went after it in earnest. "I was still a figurehead in the squadron," Taylor wrote, "a really infuriating position to be put in" (ibid.). He met Lord Balfour, the parliamentary undersecretary of state for air, to whom he complained about being double-crossed. He reminded Balfour that the press was a public witness to the promise of leadership of the squadron and now he wanted either sole command or permission to return to the Royal Navy. Sometimes, fury at officialdom works or perhaps it was the implied threat of bad publicity. At the end of January 1941, Taylor was in command of the Eagle Squadron and, a short time later, it was declared operational. Sweeney describes a visit to 71 Squadron at Kirton Lindsey at that time: "We were standing on the airfield with the CO, Bill Taylor, watching the landings," Sweeney wrote in his autobiography. "A Spitfire was coming in to land when we noticed another plane behind him; at the same time, a trail of dust snaked across the field in front of the Spitfire. It was only then that we realized that the second plane was an enemy fighter and the serpentine track of smoke and dirt was the fire pattern of his guns. Fortunately, the [German] pilot was firing in front of the Spitfire" (*Sweeney*).

Things did not go smoothly for Taylor. His experience as a commanding officer was gained in a peacetime environment with the U.S. Marine Corps Reserve Unit, Grosse Isle, Michigan, and his style probably would not have meshed easily with a band of air warriors in furious and frequent contact with the enemy. Further, traditions differ between air forces and navies. A naval commanding officer lives alone and has his own steward and cook, even having to ask permission of his officers to enter the wardroom. Taylor's Eagle Squadron, in common with most Royal Air Force fighter units, was known and tolerated for its independence of manner and easy informality. Taylor chose not to mix with the rest of his squadron, believing that a good commanding officer was a leader rather than a friend. Without doubt, he was immensely proud of the Eagle Squadron and ambitious for it to succeed. Age decided the problem without loss of face to either side.

In July 1941 Taylor was called to Group Headquarters and told that, having reached the age of thirty-six, he was now too old to take a fighter squadron into action over France. He was offered a promotion to wing commander (lieutenant colonel equivalent) and command of a fighter operational training unit; he declined and requested a transfer to the U.S. Navy. As early as the summer of 1940, the Royal Navy had informed Taylor that "in the event of the United States becoming involved in hostilities," U.S. personnel would be released to join American forces if they wished. Taylor switched uniforms again and for the last time (Rear Admiral H. Pott, RN, Naval Attaché, British Embassy, Washington, DC, to Lieutenant Taylor, RNVR, 3 August 1940, R. B. White collection).

He was re-commissioned into the U.S. Naval Reserve with the rank of lieutenant commander at the U.S. Embassy on Grosvenor Square. The Navy gave him back the same officer lineal number (60930) he had originally been assigned in 1926, a considerable benefit because the number directly affects an officer's promotion timetable. His experience with radar and British fighter direction and control was a valuable addition to American war preparations. Consequently, he was assigned to Admiral Husband Kimmel's staff at Pearl Harbor to set up fighter defenses for Oahu, Hawaii. Taylor went on to serve aboard the carriers *Yorktown*, *Wasp*, *Enterprise*, *Saratoga*, and *Ranger*. In late 1945 he commanded the Naval Air Station, Port Lyauty, in French Morocco. France awarded him the Legion of Honor in recognition of his services. His U.S. Navy fitness report at that time describes an officer who is "quiet and unassuming, but self-assured" and an "inspiration to his subordinates."

Not all bombs dropped on Britain exploded on impact. Between September 1940 and July 1941 an average of eighty-four bombs per day fell on civilian targets and failed to explode. Finding and disarming the unexploded bombs was the task of an overworked corps of military specialists whose chance of surviving the war was anything but hopeful. A newspaper article in autumn 1941 described a meeting in the cocktail lounge of London's elegant Savoy Hotel, when an RNVR lieutenant introduced himself to a group of assembled reporters. He had heard their American accents. "I'm an American, also," he said to them. He was there to celebrate; next day he was headed back to the states on thirty days' leave (Elizabeth Kauffman Bush notes, 13 September 2001; Charlotte Hammond collection).

The lieutenant watched a departing friend, a Royal Air Force fighter pilot, weave an unsteady path out of the room and mused quietly, "Get ashamed of myself every time I see those guys. Risk their lives every day. And me? I'm supposed to be a naval officer and they won't let me go to sea." After a pause he added, "Bum eyes. They threw me out of the U.S. Navy because I wear glasses." "What do you do now?" one of the reporters asked him. The officer laughed. "Oh, they've got me on shore duty," he answered, "nursing these goddam land mines." There was a long silence. The average life expectancy for a man in this line of work was seven weeks. The reporters all knew that land-mine duty in Britain took great courage and was numbered among the most deadly of all war tasks (ibid.).

By spring 1940, when Kauffman began his work, Britain had more than two thousand unexploded bombs to deal with. Disposal units were overwhelmed with assignments and attrition. During the Battle of Britain, bomb disposal squads rushed to places where huge Luftwaffe parachute bombs had fallen and not exploded. The squads roped off the impact area and then tackled the nerve-shredding task of trying to dismantle the mines and make them harmless. The lieutenant said that he had done this work for nearly a year and that his father was Rear Admiral (later, Vice Admiral) James L. Kauffman who commanded the U.S. Navy's defenses in the Gulf of Mexico.

"Eyes went bad on me just after I finished at Annapolis," he explained. "I thought maybe they'd be good enough for the Royal Navy. They are—for shore duty." The self-effacing young naval officer was Draper Laurence Kauffman (ibid.).

The Royal Navy accepted Kauffman without hesitation when he landed at Methil. His Annapolis background and a father who was a serving flag officer in the U.S. Navy spoke for him, as did his gallantry in the French army. Instead of the Royal Naval College, Kauffman went to *King Alfred* for training where he was elected class officer. The job required that he take his turn as vice president of the Mess, the captain being the president. Thursday nights were reserved for the formal "dining-in" evening when, at the end of the meal, the president calls for the loyal toast, saying, "Mr. Vice, the King!" The vice president then calls on all present to drink the toast by responding, "Gentlemen, the King!" Everyone repeats, "The King" before taking a sip of his drink, normally port. Kauffman asked his commander whether it would be in very bad taste if he amended his toast. That evening, when called upon, Kauffman said, "Gentlemen, the President and the King!" and was astounded when, without a murmur, every single diner, without fumbling, followed suit and chorused, "The President and the King."

It was at *King Alfred* that Kauffman volunteered, albeit without much enthusiasm, for bomb disposal duties (UXB). One night, the Luftwaffe had dropped a bomb that failed to detonate in the nearby town of Hove. Every man in an Army disposal squad was killed when their efforts to defuse another bomb nearby failed, resulting in a premature explosion. Not surprisingly, response was tepid in the classrooms when the Royal Navy asked the students for volunteers. In fact no one at all put himself forward. A further request produced three volunteers, but not the six men required.

A full bomb disposal team's complement numbered fifteen men. It was the job of local air raid wardens to identify the exact location of an unexploded bomb, sometimes buried as deep as sixty feet in the ground. Soldiers dug the excavations, using timbers to shore up the sides of the hole. To do the defusing, the team leader, a Bomb Disposal commissioned officer, climbed into the pit and down to where the bomb lay exposed.

The death of the Hove unit moved Kauffman to volunteer, taking his place in line for an interview with Captain Llewellyn, director of the Royal Navy's newly established Bomb Disposal Department. Kauffman felt "pretty shaky, particularly as I had just that morning, stopped at the very large hole in the ground where the time bomb had eliminated the Army squad thirty-six hours earlier. The Captain started off by asking, 'And, young man, are you frightfully keen for this type of duty?' I said, 'No, sir' and heaved a sigh of relief, for I thought that let me off the hook. But it turned out that that was the key question. Anyone who answered yes was crossed off the list immediately. The thought being that anybody who was crazy enough to be particularly keen for this type of duty was too crazy to get it" (USNI Oral History Program, May 1978 interview, #1, p. 56ff., Kauffman family archive).

In October 1940 Kauffman, now wearing green felt between his wavy gold rings to denote Special Branch, went to HM Naval Base Holyhead on the island of Anglesey in North Wales at about the same time that the Germans introduced a land mine designed to cause maximum damage to the docks of London, Liverpool, and Glasgow. With the surreal logic that only someone who has served in the military services can fully grasp, the Royal Navy retained responsibility for the disposal of all mines regardless of where they were found, however far inland.

In late November the city of Liverpool experienced a major three-night Blitz and, as Holyhead was only a few hours away by car, Kauffman found himself with the city's UXB unit. Cars assigned to this duty had crimson fenders. The whole population knew what that color meant and they were profuse in their kindness to the men who did such work. This was Britain's first experience of the enemy's use of land mines and there were nowhere near enough disposal officers to deal with the problem. Support personnel were kept at least the regulation two hundred yards distant. The unit was a little frantic, Kauffman remembered, but his assistance was welcome and he soon went to work alongside one of the other officers, Lieutenant Brian Turner Riley, who had already dealt with two mines and was considered the group's most experienced officer. Riley was awarded the George Medal for his work during this period and, in 1942, the King's Commendation for Brave Conduct.

For Kauffman the experience made an unforgettable impression not because this was his first bomb but because of its setting. When the mine came down in urban Liverpool its parachute tangled around the chimney of a house of ill repute, and the mine, around eight feet long, rested its nose in the seat of an overstuffed chair. Some early decorative Christmas streamers had come loose in the room and had wrapped themselves around the casing, lending the scene a "hilariously ludicrous aspect." Fortunately the fuse was readily accessible and the mine was quickly made safe. But not everybody had such luck. Kauffman inherited a set of defusing tools that had been the property of a couple of officers who were killed the very same morning. He also got assigned to him an outstanding naval rating, Petty Officer Martin. For the rest of the Blitz they worked together as a team and, among their other accomplishments, made harmless eight parachute mines.

Kauffman returned to the city following another pre-holiday attack. On Christmas Eve, 1940, he defused a mine that had landed in a run-down area, requiring the evacuation of a thousand people from their homes. The mine was hard to reach and it was nearly midnight before the deadly device was rendered safe and everyone could return home. Things got even harder with the next mission, early on Christmas morning, when a mine smashed into the cellar of a house, littering explosive materials throughout the ruined building.

Kauffman was back in Holyhead in early January 1941, when a parachute mine landed on the railway lines and failed to explode. It was bitterly cold as he went to work with Petty Officer Martin standing by, observing and making notes from the safety zone so he could replicate Kauffman's moves, if anything went wrong, and figure out his error. Cold is a disadvantage when doing delicate work and it made Kauffman's fingers stiff. His hands slipped and he lost his grip as he attempted to untwist the fuse. Instantly the fuse mechanism started its audible countdown tick. Kauffman hurtled away at top speed and managed to cover several yards, but the detonation when it came was near enough to blow him clean off his feet.

Petty Officer Martin timed the whole event at eleven seconds from the moment his boss jumped to his feet, along with the exact distance Kauffman covered. Kauffman was told afterward that when the bomb detonated he was right alongside a small tree and that "the tree and I left the ground simultaneously and landed together 22 feet away. I passed out" (ibid.).

Captain Currey's official report dryly noted that "it is apparent that Lieutenant Kauffman accomplished the equivalent of a nine second 100 yard dash. This world record may have been induced by a sense of urgency" (ibid.). In addition to a large bump on his head Kauffman's kidneys were damaged and he was sent to Oban, Scotland, to recuperate for several months. In March 1941 he was still convalescing in Scotland when Glasgow was severely bombed. Kauffman immediately sought permission to go to help tackle the city's UXBs. Two months later Kauffman's arrival in Plymouth coincided with the Luftwaffe's bombing of that city in a seemingly unending series of raids. For five of the first eight nights he spent there, Kauffman was a busy man.

Prime Minister Winston Churchill took a personal interest in UXB work and it was under his direction that the Bomb Disposal organization became an efficient and capable force. When war began, bomb disposal had been the responsibility of small units of Sappers (Army engineers), each unit led by a junior noncommissioned officer. Much more was needed, and Churchill quickly saw to the establishment of a vastly expanded system that trained expert personnel who could benefit from immediate technical intelligence about German ordnance fuses and explosive device construction. Kauffman described how the prime minister himself came to inspect his unit. "He had, of course, been briefed by aides and so he came to me and he asked me—I mean he knew that I was an American and said, 'How did you happen to join our Navy?' He actually spent about fifteen or twenty minutes with me and that was a very long time." And Churchill remembered because later, when the elder Kauffman was head of the Allied Antisubmarine Board set up by Churchill and Roosevelt, Churchill asked him at a luncheon, "Tell me, Admiral, how did you feel about your son doing mine-disposal work over here in England?" (ibid.).

Kauffman's performance earned him a commendation for "brave conduct and devotion to duty in connection with an unexploded parachute mine" (*London Gazette,* June 6, 1941) of which he sent his father a copy together with the orders detailing his promotion to temporary, acting, probationary lieutenant. "Dad underlined 'temp,' 'prob,' 'act' and then slashed a line across the paper in red, and wrote, also in red, 'Cautious people, the British.'" As July 1941 approached the BBC wanted to broadcast a message from Kauffman. They ran a publicity photograph with the comment, "Lieutenant Draper Kauffman tells of his impressions of wartime Britain from Trafalgar Square, London, on Independence Day" (ibid.).

On July 4 he broadcast:

> Hello America. Believe it or not the British are celebrating the 4th July this year—but without fireworks. They have too much of that over here normally. These Limies are a really grand crowd. You have all read and heard how they can take it. Well, it honestly has to be seen to be believed. It is tragic yet horribly inspiring. Incidentally, they are all very grateful for help coming over from home, and treat all of us who are serving over here like kings in spite of the very small part we are doing as yet. Their appreciation is amazing in a way, because it seems to me that it is we who should be grateful to them for the wonderful way they are mending the Anglo-American front line and keeping a barrier between the Huns and ourselves. (ibid.)

Two defusings in particular stayed in Kauffman's memory. One was the disposal of an acoustic fuse where the slightest sound (a cough, a wrench knocking a bolt) would set off the detonation. Unscrewing the fuse had to be done a quarter turn at a time, followed by three minutes of waiting. Each quarter turn was reported by telephone in order to record the exact number of turns. If the UXB exploded prematurely, killing the officer, there was at least an accurate record. The next man faced with a similar defusing would know how much progress had been achieved before the detonation. It was slow, nerve-wracking work. The other unforgettable UXB was nicknamed "The George." This was in summer 1941 and it was to be his last job in England. The George was an especially nasty refinement on a 1,000-kilogram bomb that had been dropped without a parachute. Working thirty feet down at the bottom of a wet hole Kauffman at first could find no obvious fuse. When he did identify the fuse, he called it the "top hat" for its shape. British scientists were fairly sure the trigger was a photoelectric cell that was ultrasensitive to light. The smallest glimmer of light would trigger the detonation. What remained of the man who had been in the crater would be so infinitesimally small that only birds could see the pieces, it was said.

Kauffman needed to work in complete darkness. "By carefully and very gently feeling around, I came across a wire and snipped it. I distinctly remember that in at least two cases I cut a wire twice, since I couldn't see." The top hat was made of heavy metal and was awkward to handle, particularly down in that hole. The four hours it took to do the work "seemed like 40 hours" (ibid.; Barbara Kauffman Bush, *America's First Frogman*, Annapolis: Naval Institute Press, 2004).

After his Independence Day broadcast Kauffman spent three weeks writing a paper on organizing UXB units in the U.S. Army and U.S. Navy. This was the genesis of the American military's Explosive Ordnance Disposal program that continues to the present day. Shortly afterward, Kauffman got news that he was to be given thirty days' home leave and it was about this time he was in the cocktail lounge of the Savoy with the Royal Air Force friend and the American journalists. He returned to the United States on the Canadian destroyer HMCS *Assiniboine*.

When the ship left Scotland the Lord Provost of Glasgow sent Kauffman's family a telegram, "Your brave son homeward bound. Glasgow thanks him for his many life saving services and congratulates you on his devotion to democracy." In October 1941 Draper Kauffman resigned from the Royal Navy to take up a lieutenant's commission in the U.S. Naval Reserve with orders to report to the Bureau of Ordnance, in Washington, D.C. He arrived with no intention whatever of transferring to the U.S. Navy, as his father wanted; he was convinced that America was not going to enter the war. But he found a country that was rapidly rearming and he changed his mind. The elder Kauffman had paved the way, "There will be no difficulty in your transferring," he told his son, "and you will not be put in the supply corps or made a civil engineer to dig ditches. Also, you will be transferred at the same rank you hold in the RNVR. I have discussed this with Admiral Nimitz, the chief of the Bureau of Personnel" (USNI Oral History Program, May 1978 interview, #1).

After the Japanese attack on Pearl Harbor, Kauffman was sent to Hawaii where he defused an unexploded 500-pound bomb in Schofield Barracks. The action brought him the award of the Navy Cross, the U.S. Navy's highest award for gallantry, second only to the Medal of Honor. His father had been awarded the same decoration in World War I. Kauffman pioneered the U.S. Navy's Explosive Ordnance Disposal School. By 1943 the school was well established. Some of the EOD recruiting officers impressed their candidates by telling them that the school had two mottos, "Our graduates are scattered all over the world" and "Be calm or be collected" (ibid.; Bush, *America's First Frogman*).

David van Epps preceded Kauffman by only a few weeks. Based on date of arrival, the first three Americans to put on a Royal Navy uniform in World War II (not including the men who are commemorated in the Painted Hall plaque) were Taylor, van Epps, and Kauffman. However, none of these men were "sea-officers" as the Greenwich plaque stipulates. Kauffman was Special Branch and the other two were Fleet Air Arm pilots. None of them stood bridge watches.

Van Epps was young and keen as mustard. He, too, skipped the Royal Naval College by training at HMS *Raven*, a shore facility that the Luftwaffe often raided and once claimed to have sunk. The Nazi propaganda mill routinely lived up to its reputation for unintended buffoonery. After being commissioned at *Raven* and further training at HMS *Heron* at RAF Station Yeovilton, he was assigned to 809 Squadron as a fighter pilot. The squadron was embarked on the carrier HMS *Victorious* protecting convoys bound for northern Russia. Van Epps also flew strike missions over German-occupied Norway. In early July 1941 he crashed his Fairey Fulmar on *Victorious*' deck. A photograph survives of the incident. His comments at the time of the accident are "unprintable." Nothing dampened his celebration of Independence Day.

On July 4 the carrier's Royal Marine band played American tunes and at 1230 the wardroom raised a toast to the United States. The band played

"The Star Spangled Banner." There were two other American citizens present, pilots who had delivered a couple of Grumman Martlets to *Victorious*. Royal Navy Workshop Artificer Stan Filmer, from Walton-on-the-Naze, played the piano. That evening, the three Americans threw their own party for the wardroom.

Van Epps was a lieutenant commander and 894 Squadron's commanding officer when he transferred to the U.S. Army Air Corps. He became commanding officer of D Flight, 4th U.S. Fighter Group. On April 9, 1944, he was reported missing in action while escorting a bombing attack on Germany. The 334th Squadron's planned takeoff had been delayed due to bad visibility and low cloud ceiling. The mission, target support, was changed. The squadron strafed two grass airfields to the south of Osnabrück. Their reports noted a dummy aircraft and one *Focke Wulf* 190. Light antiaircraft flak was experienced at both places. Captain Van Epps pulled up to one thousand feet after the final attack and was not seen again. Epps spent the remainder of the conflict as a prisoner of war at *Stalag Luft* I. He was released from captivity on May 1, 1945, and repatriated the next day.

John Edward Hampson was first assigned to the Royal Navy aerodrome at HMS *Daedalus*, Lee-on-the-Solent, where many civilian pilots were retrained to naval standards. The school was equipped with a veritable museum of dated aircraft types; in the twenty-first century it reads like an aviation museum inventory list: Hart Trainer, Osprey, Nimrod, Shark, Swordfish, Proctor, Hornet, Moth, Gipsy Moth, Tiger Moth, and Vega Gull. In April 1941, flying with 780 Squadron, Hampson collided with a Percival Proctor. In late December, with 772 Squadron at HMS *Landrail*, Scotland, he crashed a Blackburn Skua. Hampson's luck held but his aircraft was a write-off. He then went to 780 Squadron with the dull but necessary mission of target-towing, height-finding exercises, photography, and radar calibration. The squadron's Walrus aircraft were also attached for air-sea rescue duty over a large area, one aircraft being required to stand by from dawn to dusk daily to pluck luckless souls out of the sea. It was important, if unromantic, work.

By early spring 1942 Hampson was out of the British Isles entirely, stationed with HMS *Goshawk*, a very distant Royal Navy observer school based in Trinidad, British West Indies.

U-boat successes were high in the western hemisphere, especially after America's entry into the war. About 95 percent of U.S. oil passed from Gulf of Mexico ports to refineries on the East Coast.

Consequently, the Caribbean provided a rich hunting ground to attack traffic in the Gulf as well as the Straits of Florida. Tanker destruction became a major U-boat objective and many ships were lost. Hampson had a job to do. After June 1942 he disappears from records.

John Stilwell was an observer in the Fleet Air Arm, a job known in the U.S. Navy as Naval Flight Officer or, popularly, "Backseater." His part of the war was fought from landing fields in Northern Ireland.

Perhaps the most independent-spirited, casually eccentric volunteer in the group was Peter Morison. Military bearing, bright buttons, and sharply creased trousers were not his strong points, nor was he much concerned by their absence. Morison was indifferent to the manner in which a junior was expected to interact with his military superiors of even very senior rank. His unaffected nonchalance toward military decorum became legendary. Only in a world war can such a free spirit survive without being hung, shot, or exiled by some irate admiral whose ego has just been crushed by the sight of the shabbily attired, cavalier young American cheerfully ambling past in British uniform, unconcerned with standard military courtesies. After some "polishing" at Royal Naval College, Morison was assigned to Royal Naval Air Station Hatston, in Orkney, where he became the Air Transport Communications officer of 782 Squadron.

But Morison disliked flying and never went up, not with his own or anyone else's squadron. Not in British aircraft or, as best as can be determined, in the military aircraft of his mother country.

Kenneth Bartlett was a noncommissioned officer at RAF Fighter Sector Headquarters where his work brought him into frequent contact with Morison. Sixty years later a bemused Bartlett recalled Morison as a friendly, jovial fellow who treated everyone alike regardless of rank. On one unforgettable occasion Morison acknowledged the senior admiral at the Scapa Flow naval base with a cheerful "Hiya, Ad!" accompanied by a casual flip of the right hand approximating a salute in the direction of his hat.

Bartlett, fearing an instant explosion, accorded the admiral an especially smart Royal Air Force salute. The admiral went on his way unperturbed but his accompanying staff grumbled audibly. They noted that Lieutenant Morison did not cut a fine figure in his blues and, indeed, it looked as if the uniform had done double duty as pajamas. It was also observed with a growl that his buttons and the gold wire of his gold cap badge had weathered into a clear shade of green.

"Prowling the passageways again, I see," Morison cheerfully hailed an astonished admiral one morning as they passed each other in the corridor (Eric Berryman, notes from conversations with Sam Morison). In August 1943 Morison transferred to the U.S. Army Air Corps where he was given an equivalent rank, that of an Army captain. It is tempting to think that his appearance did not overly benefit from the change of uniform and insignia. Peter Morison was the last of the U.S. citizens to be commissioned into the Royal Navy.

Action in Other Theaters

Allied leadership prepared for the main invasion of the European Continent with a series of amphibious operations elsewhere on enemy-occupied terrain. In mid-August 1942 the raid on the French port of Dieppe, Operation Jubilee, was meant to test capabilities, shock the Germans, and boost civilian morale in Britain as well as in France; it did none of these. Carl Konow aboard HMT *Prince Leopold* was tasked to embark a group of Canadian raiders. Unlikely hulls that had been designed for strictly peacetime purposes were pressed into military service due to demand on a global scale and losses to U-boat torpedoes. Thus, *Prince Leopold*, the grandly re-designated ex–Belgian State Railway ferry built in 1929, was converted into a lightly armed troop carrier. Often the target of strafing by the Luftwaffe, *Prince Leopold* trained for her mission in landing exercises with Canadian troops off England's south coast, near the Solent where Henry VIII had watched an early version of poor design on its maiden voyage, *Mary Rose*, "turn turtle" and sink like a stone with the loss of five hundred lives.

In Southampton, Lord Louis Mountbatten boarded HMT *Prince Leopold* to give her crew and embarked soldiers a pep talk before they went into action. Mountbatten was chief of Combined Operations at the time, which meant that he had charge of commando initiatives like the one that was about to sweep up Konow and John Parker's oldest son, Frank. On August 18, 1942, she took aboard three hundred men with their equipment and the eight small landing craft they needed to reach enemy beaches.

The English Channel crossing went to plan. Mines had been swept and a safe passage marked with red and green buoys. At 0300 the next day, *Prince Leopold* delivered her cargo of troops at the launch point and returned without incident. She may have been the last Allied vessel to leave unscathed. Most everyone else had it infinitely tougher. It was only long after the war that the full casualty figures could be revealed. Of nearly 5,000 Canadians in the operation less than half, 2,210, made it back to England and many of them were wounded. Altogether there were 3,367 casualties, including 1,946 prisoners of war. More than 900 Canadians gave their lives. The Royal Air Force and Royal Canadian Air Force lost 119 aircraft, the highest single-day total of the entire war. There was also a small U.S. Ranger contingent at Dieppe, the first Americans to see action against Germans on land. Of these U.S. Rangers, three were killed in action and eight were wounded (Jim DeFelice, *Rangers at Dieppe*, New York: Berkley Caliber, 2008).

In Canada, survivors of the Dieppe raid are given the same kind of reverence accorded in the United States to veterans of the Bataan Death March, and in Britain to those who survived Japanese captivity elsewhere. The best face that can be put on the debacle is that the raid taught valuable lessons that were applied to great effect in planning Operation Overlord two years later. Amphibious assault planning and execution never repeated the scale of Dieppe failures. Among the changes the Allied commanders introduced were newly formed Royal Navy Commando units specially trained to land ahead of the first invasion assault to clear beaches, remove mines and underwater obstructions, and gather intelligence about enemy strength. Several of the U.S. personnel who served in the Royal Navy spent time in units like these. Draper Kauffman became a U.S. Navy commando and "frogman" scouting hostile beaches in the Pacific islands campaign. Derek Lee took part in British commando operations in Malaya and Burma, and Kittredge was a commando in North Africa, Sicily, Normandy, and, continuing in that role, had been posted to the Far East in preparation for the invasion of Japan's home islands when the war ended.

For Operation Torch, the invasion of North Africa in November 1942 (the first joint Anglo-American landing of the war), there were four hundred–plus British commandos. Why Kittredge came to volunteer for such hazardous employment is not known but he was assigned to Beach Command E (for

Easy), which formed at Inverary and Coulport House, Scotland. Three units, C (reformed after heavy losses at Dieppe), F, and G, together with part of H and J landed with the first assault elements and took immediate charge of the African beaches. After eliminating snipers the commandos dug slit trenches for protection and set up machine guns.

Their primary task was to guide ashore 29,000 troops, 2,400 vehicles, and 14,000 tons of supplies on three different invasion beaches. Working with U.S. assault troops, Kittredge arrived in the uniform of his mother country because British commandos had been issued American uniforms to placate French troops who were suspicious of the British. The gesture failed utterly. Vichy French forces fought briskly for three days and inflicted more than 2,000 casualties. French anger is not difficult to explain in the aftermath of Churchill's order to attack the French fleet at Mers el Kebir in 1940. Even into the new millennium, France remains angry and acutely sensitive about the incident and has never ceased to disavow there was ever an intention to let their fleet serve the Nazis. Anger was still white-hot during Operation Torch.

In July 1943 came Operation Husky, the invasion of Sicily, which was launched to knock Italy out of the war. Operation Husky was Kittredge's second invasion. He wrote:

> On the 9th of July we steamed on to the ill-fated island. By sundown we could see Mt. Etna in the distance, which didn't seem exactly fitting somehow. Everything appeared too much out in the open and above-board. Not enough foul play. However, after dark the likelihood of foul play appeared entirely plausible, as is often the case. Morale, incidentally was excellent. I stood on deck all evening and when a flight of bombers went over us en route to Syracuse we knew the thing was on—though we weren't to land for a long while, the sight was most stirring. ("Here's a Vivid Account of Sicily Landing," *Cincinnati Times-Star*, 4 September 1945, Edmund Skip Kittridge papers)

Kittredge came ashore on the island only to discover he was on the wrong beach. As he started to walk across a small vineyard to his assigned area, "Bang! Down I go." He had triggered an antipersonnel mine. "I knew immediately what had hit me and my first thought (after calling 'Help! Help!' entirely instinctively like a fool) was what a great clown I was not to look for anti-personnel mines here. Indeed, when I opened my eyes and looked about me while lying on the ground the first thing I saw was another unexploded mine about ten feet away" (ibid.).

The type of mine that got him was detonated by trip wires strung low along the ground, virtually invisible. "The thing went off about a yard from me," he said, "and got my legs, chiefly the left knee, which had three holes about the size of quarters in it. I couldn't walk and so just lay there and mopped away the blood . . . and watched the shelling of the craft on the beach 200 to 300 yards away. Those soldiers, incidentally, were disembarking absolutely indifferent to the shells plopping in the water ten, twenty-five or thirty yards from them . . . nothing bothered those fellows in the least. There's something in this British reserve we all heard so much about." Kittredge wrote to his family, "I was taken on a stretcher to the dressing station and eventually in the afternoon was put in a patch near the beach with other casualties. I never spent a more pleasant afternoon than I did lying out there under the almond trees in the sun day-dreaming, musing and watch Jerries' exceedingly unsuccessful bombings of our ships just off the beaches" (ibid.). German aim was to improve.

A stretcher carried Kittredge to a hospital ship, the aging and converted SS *Talamba*. On the same day the ship was attacked in broad daylight and sunk with the loss of five lives. Kittredge recounts, "The nurse was putting a new dressing on my knee when—glory be!—there was a short whistle, a bang and a terrific clatter of breaking glass. I assured the nurse it was a small bomb and would do so large a ship little harm. Fifteen minutes later another whistle, bang and shower of broken glass. After I don't know how long—perhaps an hour—the ship heeled quickly and sharply to starboard. An English lad helped me out of my battle dress jacket and we let ourselves down some lines into the water—which felt exceedingly pleasant, soothing and nice" (ibid.).

His luck held. Kittredge was pulled aboard a destroyer that came to rescue survivors. "Somebody gave me an oilskin coat. I lay down on deck and was asleep in five minutes." Later, he bemoaned the British army's lack of seamanship knowledge. "I've still stray bits of metal in me. They are not necessarily intending to take all the bits and pieces out of me, although I tell them they must, for it won't do for a naval officer to have metal in him, inasmuch as it will throw the compass off if he gets near one" (ibid.).

Kittredge's commando unit returned from Italy to Great Britain at the end of October and, following a period of leave, was billeted in Gailes, Scotland. Kittredge, however, remained in the Royal Navy hospital at Chatham for many weeks; he eventually recovered and was returned to active service.

After service with HM *LSE 50*, a repair tender for surface ships damaged by enemy action and heavy usage, Konow joined the crew of a brand-new vessel. On February 15, 1943, in New Orleans as the first lieutenant he put HM *LST 198* into commission. She was the second of 157 LSTs constructed by Chicago Bridge & Iron Company: in the small town of Seneca, Illinois, on the Illinois River, in the heart of cornfield country. Before the war the company had never before built ships. At 4,000 tons fully loaded and 328 feet long, the design incorporated a flat bottom hull to allow deep penetration of the beach and bow doors that opened to discharge men, their tanks, and trucks. While in New Orleans, Konow took the whole crew ashore for ham and eggs.

After the "shakedown cruise" in the Mississippi Delta the ship sailed to Norfolk, Virginia, then New York City where she was fitted with radar. She spent a month in Boston before heading to Nova Scotia and joining a convoy across the Atlantic. Routed through Liverpool to be unloaded and have her bow doors unwelded, the ship steamed through the Straits of Gibraltar into the Mediterranean. The commanding officer was Commander Gordon Benjamin Rudyerd-Helpman, RN, who was awarded Britain's Distinguished Service Cross for his courage, leadership, and skill in the assault on Anzio and for helping to maintain an unbroken flow of supplies to the invasion beachhead. Konow could not have had a better mentor.

In Operation Husky HM *LST 198* was attacked by an Italian torpedo bomber, but the pilot misjudged the ship's draft and the torpedo went under the starboard stern of the ship and came out on the port side. On July 10, 1943, D-day at Salerno, cannon shells ripped through the hull and the ship took many casualties. HM *LST 198* claimed one enemy aircraft shot down. In a letter to U.S. General George Marshall in 1943 referring to the challenges of organizing the Italian campaign, Churchill worried, "The whole of this difficult question only arises out of the absurd shortage of LSTs." The excruciatingly slow top speed of eleven knots made the crew feel very vulnerable indeed. With wry humor, Rear Admiral Samuel E. Morison explained that

LSTs "were literally what their crews called them, 'Large, Slow Targets.'" Echoing Churchill, he added that LSTs were "the most useful of all-round craft invented by the Navy" (Morison, *The Two Ocean War*, Boston: Little, Brown, 1963).

When he arrived at the port of Syracuse, which had just been captured by British forces, Konow went ashore to ask headquarters where to deliver the ship's cargo of tanks. After initially defending terrain only lightly, German army resistance in Sicily stiffened and the more Allied armor, the better. Inside headquarters, Konow heard angry voices coming from the other side of the conference room door. Minutes later, a rear admiral stormed out, followed by an army lieutenant general, argument still in full cry. Undeterred, Konow approached the two men, excused himself and asked where the admiral would like his tanks brought. At this, the general interrupted and with a smile said, "Ah, MY tanks!" Whereupon the admiral glowered and replied at once, "Then you can just leave them anywhere" (extracts, radio interview "Life of Karl Konow," Copenhagen, 12 January 1970, Carl Konow family collection).

The army officer was Bernard Law Montgomery, later, Field Marshal 1st Viscount Montgomery of El 'Alamain, who commanded all British ground forces. The admiral was Sir Rhoderick Robert McGrigor, then flag officer, Sicily, who went on to become Admiral of the Fleet and First Sea Lord, Britain's operational head of the Royal Navy. McGrigor knew about transporting tanks in local waters. As head of Force B transporting 51 Highland Division to the Pachino Peninsular, he had likely witnessed HM *LST 547* capsize in heavy seas with the loss of six Sherman tanks. And he might have seen the breakdown of several other LSTs and the total loss of another to fire.

After Syracuse and Salerno, Operation Avalanche, on September 9, 1943, Konow's ship participated in the landings at Anzio, Operation Shingle, on January 22, 1944, where Ferris was blinded. Ex-Signalman F. E. Hart remembered the Anzio D-day "was very quiet but it wasn't long before the German counterattack, when the troops got pinned down for several weeks." It was only after the troops broke out of the beachhead and Rome was captured that Konow's LST sailed for England. Hart wrote, "On arriving in the UK each watch was given seven days leave. We then sailed for Harwich and waited for the signal for D-Day." Normandy followed. He added, "As the troops advanced we delivered a special assignment to Amsterdam. We were told the crates contained the furniture for the surrender meeting" (F. E. Hart, former crew member, letters to R. E. White, Charlotte Hammond collection).

Derek Lee left the Atlantic to serve in the Far East in a series of hazardous, clandestine assignments. Precisely how he came to leave shipboard life for an elite commando corps is not clear, but family lore says it was somehow connected to his prewar status as a second level (*nidan*) black belt in judo, and someone from the FBI or OSS who made contact with him in 1944 when he was home on leave in New York City. Just like Kittredge, Lee traded the relative luxuries of life on a warship in the open ocean for a perilous existence much nearer the enemy. Promoted to lieutenant commander, on May 4, 1944, Lee was seconded by the Royal Navy to the Office of Strategic Services, forerunner of the Central Intelligence Agency, in the China-Burma-India Theater.

For the rest of the war, he led a commando unit that paddled and swam through shark-infested, sea snake–rich tropical waters to get a close look at the Imperial Japanese Army in its jungle environment. Lee lived the kind of action-packed, combat-filled life of improbable dangers and thrills found in schoolboy pulp fiction or over-the-top Hollywood films. Attached to Allied Land Forces, South East Asia in their advance down the Burma coast, Lee was the deputy commanding officer of the overall Commando Operational Group, and commanding officer of a maritime unit of Royal Marine and American military and native personnel. Lee personally planned and led sixteen clandestine infiltrations of enemy territory in a series of daring reconnaissance missions with operational code names like South Dakota, Boston, Wellington, and Target. His job was to penetrate Japanese positions ashore to gain information about the local geography and geology, as well as the enemy's strength and defenses. He worked chiefly at night. Lee's team used kayaks and native craft to infiltrate and retrieve agents and gather tactical details.

On August 8, 1945, Lee took under his command an American naval officer along with three native agents and parachuted with them into enemy-occupied Malaya to gain intelligence for proposed landings on the Malaya coast. In Operation Wellington, Lee and his OSS commandos left HMS *Newcastle* steaming over the horizon, to land on Cheduba Island. Two radio operators remained at the beachhead while Lee and a staff sergeant went inland to report enemy dispositions, the attitude of the natives, the potable water supply, condition of roads and other tactical details, and to recruit natives to their side.

In the second phase of the operation a few days later, he went ashore in a canoe in advance of all other forces to obtain hydrographic information on the proposed landing beaches, the number of Japanese troops, and their garrison locations. The work of Lee's OSS party is credited with being "directly responsible for the success of the Kyauknimaw landings." For Operation Target, Lee made a night swim to a Japanese-held coast in order to assist British forces to land heavy guns and bring the enemy under direct shellfire.

A kayak party penetrated ten to twelve miles inside "strongly-held Japanese territory" to make a study of the waterways. They discovered a couple of well-built log blocks completely barring the *chaung* as an avenue of entry (*chaung* is the local name for the innumerable narrow tidal channels, or waterways, intersecting the low-lying, jungle-covered Burmese coastal plain). The traps were covered by shore-based Japanese troops strategically positioned between the two blocks. Also, Japanese motor launches patrolled the *chaung* and numerous Japanese shore parties and sentries were discovered all along the mangrove fringe bordering the *chaung*.

Skillful and intrepid maneuvering helped Lee and his men to elude the enemy and bring back the required information. Operation South Dakota got Lee near enough to the Japanese encampment to hear them conversing. Despite the close proximity of the enemy, the commandos were able to make a minute inspection of every facet of the heavily constructed log blocks obstructing the *chaung*, including an underwater inspection, before paddling away. They also took soundings of the entire length of the canoe trip. The total party was one officer, Lee, and three men who carried only sidearms. The entire mission was without hope of support, rescue, or assistance if discovered.

Among the family's many stories about Lee's exploits, there are two of particular note. An accidental grenade detonation was a serious infraction because the consequences could be dire indeed, divulging their position as well as suffering potential casualties. No one among the natives in the unit confessed to being responsible, so Lee consulted with the local authorities and together it was decided to apply a "lie detector." Their version of a polygraph consisted of a pot of boiling water with a knife at the bottom. Each man would coat his hands and forearms with axle grease and reach into the pot to pull the knife clear of the water and then return the knife to the bottom of the pot. Lee was the first to demonstrate the procedure and show that a man telling the truth would not have to worry about getting scalded by the boiling water. The men started going through the line when one of them began to scream in pain before even touching the water. This was the man who had triggered the grenade.

On another occasion, Lee was on a mission to clear a small landing spot for a parachute drop. He had with him an early form of plastic explosives and was not familiar with their power. He reasoned, "If I use half the amount and I don't get the desired effect, the other half will be rendered somewhat useless." With that, he put all fifty pounds at the base of a tree and withdrew to a safe distance. As he put it, "When all the debris had settled, and my ears had stopped ringing, I realized we could probably have landed a B-29" (Derek Lee papers).

For operations Akron, Zebra, Ardmore, Yoke, and Ruth, Lee transported native agents down the Burma coast in OSS patrol boats and directed their infiltration into enemy territory. On several occasions he actually took the agents ashore personally in small rubber life rafts at great risk and danger to himself, "since on each of these occasions he landed on Japanese-held territory well beyond any support in event of detection," Lee's superior noted. In its review of these commando exploits, Headquarters, U.S. Armed Forces, Ceylon noted that Lee never hesitated to accept extremely hazardous assignments, and that he personally "led the men under his command successfully through all dangerous missions with great skill and courage." Headquarters also applauded Lee's excellent seamanship and praised his judgment, which was always cool and calculated. This capable American in a British naval officer's uniform was assessed as a first-rate leader who met his mission obligations with daring and tactical acuity. The U.S. military command awarded Lee the Legion of Merit; Britain awarded him the King's Medal for Courage for having carried out thirty-two operations (Joint Chiefs of Staff, Office of Strategic Services [6/13/1942–10/01/1945] ARC 2178650 / MLR A1 224, U.S. NARA).

Leggat was also in the Pacific War during this same period. He had switched to American forces in March 1944, and with his valuable sea time and specialized seagoing tickets the U.S. Navy promoted him to lieutenant and gave him command of USS *LCS (L) 44*. LCS (L) ships were shallow-draft amphibious vessels specifically designed to crawl right up a Japanese-occupied beach, land its cargo of infantry, and provide covering fire using machine guns and rocket fire. In May 1945 Leggat's gallantry brought him the award of the Bronze Star Medal for his actions against Japanese forces during amphibious operations in the Tarakan, North Borneo, campaign. When survivors from a sunken mine-sweeper drifted toward the enemy's beach, Leggat immediately went to their aid. Under hostile fire, he unhesitatingly took his ship across known minefields to within five hundred yards of the hostile beach and, hurling the full strength of his batteries at the Japanese emplacements ashore, rescued the survivors from under the enemy's guns.

Surgeon Lieutenant Francis Mason Hayes died when HMS Veteran *was lost with all hands west of Ireland, a torpedo casualty. Hayes had just celebrated his thirtieth birthday. He left a young widow and a five-year-old son. (John Peter Hayes collection)*

Oswald Birrel Deiter, commanding officer of HMML 115. *(June and John Wallace collection)*

Perhaps the most idealistic of the volunteers, 6'4" tall William Perkins Homans with the "giant Apache face" was physically imposing, raw-boned, broad-shouldered, and enormously gifted. He wanted to be a fighter pilot but his great size defeated the cockpit. His post-war career as an attorney made American legal history. (Homans family collection)

Promoted to commander, RNVR Alex Henry Cherry was assigned to HMS Royal Katherine, *the Royal Navy's headquarters in occupied Germany. His exceptional staff officer skills earned him high praise and award of the Order of the British Empire (Military Division). (Michael Sabatell family collection)*

Henry Fremont Ripley graduated with the U.S. Naval Academy, class of 1926. In 1941 he resigned his regular commission in the U.S. Navy to volunteer as a junior officer in the Royal Navy. He served on Canadian corvettes assigned to the North Atlantic. (Courtesy of Special Collections & Archives Department, United States Naval Academy)

Sub-lieutenant Edwin Fairman Russell under way on the flying bridge aboard the heavy cruiser HMS Norfolk. *In a letter to his relative, Prime Minister Winston Churchill, he wrote, "events justified my enlisting in a 'foreign' service and proud to have been allowed to have served such a gallant people." (Serena Balfour collection)*

Lady Sarah Spencer-Churchill and Edwin Russell (right) on their wedding day in 1943. When his daughter Serena was born at Blenheim Palace the 10th Duke of Marlborough, Russell's father-in-law, sent his kinsman Winston Churchill twelve plover eggs. The grandson, also named Winston Churchill, helped to organize the 2001 plaque rededication; in the photograph he is the three-year-old boy page, second from left. (Serena Balfour collection)

The headline read "Recruit from the USA. At least one American has already joined our Forces. Captain [William Erwin Gibson] Taylor came to England a fortnight before the outbreak of war. And he has been enlisted now in the Fleet Air Arm." (National Air & Space Museum, Smithsonian Institution)

"Temporary, Probationary, Acting" Lieutenant Draper Laurence Armitage Kauffman, RNVR, was decorated for bravery for defusing an unexploded parachute mine. On his return to the United States, the Lord Provost of Glasgow sent Kauffman's family a telegram: "Your brave son homeward bound. Glasgow thanks him for his many life saving services and congratulates you on his devotion to democracy." (Kauffman family collection)

David Arnold van Epps (in duffel coat) as commanding officer of 894 Squadron. (Sheena Taylor collection)

David van Epps, a fighter pilot with 809 Squadron embarked on HMS Victorious. *Van Epps' Fairey Fulmar, seen here, crashed on deck in early July 1941. He had left his mic open and his language is said to have blistered paint. The mishap did nothing to dampen his celebration of Independence Day. (Courtesy of Fleet Air Arm Museum, Yeovilton)*

For service aboard HMS Sardonyx *Lieutenant Derek Lee was cited for gallantry and mentioned in despatches. Later in his sea officer career he was appointed first lieutenant of HMS* Bickerton. *As the intrepid commanding officer of a unit of Anglo-American commandos, Derek Lee operated in the teeth of Japanese forces in the Far East and was decorated with the Legion of Merit and the King's Medal for Courage. (Davis Lee collection and Diana Pritchard collection)*

On D-day George Hoague Jr. was credited with sinking twenty-five U.S. and Allied ships off the Normandy coast to form a vital artificial harbor for the invasion. Seen here with his daughter Daphne. (Courtesy Hearst Publications)

Californian John Matthew Leggat was one of the few American volunteers who missed the Royal Naval College. He got his training at HMS Drake *before reporting to HMS* Woolston, *motto: "Where Our Forefathers Lead We Follow." (U.S. Navy)*

HM LST 301 *firmly on French ground during the invasion of Europe, June 1944. She delivered cargo to Normandy on D-day. In April 1942, Leggat went to HMS* King Alfred *for more schooling and then to sea with* LST 301. *There were never enough LSTs in the whole war. "All turned upon LSTs," wrote Winston Churchill. (Imperial War Museum)*

The Painted Hall where Admiral Nelson's body lay in state after the Battle of Trafalgar and where the plaque was laid honoring U.S. volunteers. (Published with permission of the Greenwich Foundation)

7 Normandy: The End Draws Near

When Britain went on a war footing in 1939, ordinary life with its sweetness of familiar routines vanished. Conditions quickly worsened. Following the debacle at Dunkirk, Hitler's Operation Sea Lion plan to invade England looked all but certain. U.S. Ambassador Kennedy loudly, gleefully predicted an imminent Nazi conquest. Disaster struck from all directions. U-boats throttled the food supply and bombers tried to obliterate cities, ports and—worse—the people's will to continue. Life abruptly became pinched and cold, the hunger layered with unending anxiety.

Subsistence depended on whatever scant quantities the government's ration stamps permitted for meat and bread, clothing and heating. An adult's weekly shopping list shrank to an allowance of two ounces each of jam and cheese and four ounces of bacon among other, equally scarce, commodities. Some things disappeared completely; bananas vanished from the table and could not be had again until long after V-E day. Virtually every household had someone in a uniform somewhere about whom they wondered and worried. Life as it had once been was pretty well forgotten. Expectations of relief had no real conviction. Rumors abounded but hope lived on, however dimly lit.

There was faith that things would improve and even, after a time, that the enemy would not prevail. The American deputy commander for the Mulberry artificial harbor project on D-day, Commander Alfred Stanford, USNR, had this to say: "There had to be an invasion, a second front. The Quebec conference in July [1943] had settled that. There had to be unconditional surrender to its irresistible force when it came. It would be bloody. There would be a new terror of losing kin and sweethearts. It would be a convulsive upheaval of an outraged humanity, with sweat and pain and dying. But people looked forward to that. It was action, not passive endurance. It meant coming closer to the time men hardly dared think of: peacetime" (Alfred Stanford, *Force Mulberry*, Whitehead Press, 2007).

People began to believe the lyrics as Vera Lynn sang, "When the lights go on again all over the world."

The population braced itself for the long haul and spiced its indomitable fortitude with wry good humor. Thurza Blurton remembered a particularly bad night in Greenwich when "bombs were dropping fast and furious. They were chucking everything down that night . . . the three of us were chatting in the shelter. We talked about this and that to try and take our minds off the bombing . . . when . . . suddenly Connie screamed. Mum said, 'Don't worry love, we're all here together.' (Meaning if we got killed, we would all go together.) 'It's not that,' Connie cried pointing to the pile of blankets which served as our communal bed, 'There's a mouse in there!' " (Thurza Blurton, "Memories: A Child in Lewisham," BBC, *WW2 People's War*, 18 March 2004).

Waiting for the "All Clear" to sound, people sat in their shelters defiant and determined to not let this assault on their life crush their spirit. The Blitz, meant to demoralize and weaken the population, had an opposite effect. People even lampooned the enemy with ribaldry:

> Hitler has only got one ball,
> Göring has two but very small,
> Himmler has something similar,
> But poor old Göbbels has no balls at all.
>
> *Anonymous. Sung to the tune of "Colonel Bogey March"*

Commander Stanford continued, "The invasion would end this long crumbling at the edges of the certainty that was England. It had to come. Since 1939 there had been ever more patience required, ever-new fortitude and sacrifice in the face of one more defeat. There must someday come the time for action, not defense. Sea gulls soaring above the London barrage balloons told the people anew that ancient belief they all held so instinctively, that the way lay across the water. An army one day would fight again in France. War could be won only by armies. But the army must be placed in France across that water" (*Force Mulberry*).

The solution to bring the great bloodletting to an end evolved into Operation Overlord, the catchall code name for the invasion. Operation Neptune was code name for the actual beach landing on Normandy. H-hour was the moment the first infantry foot touched French sand on D-day. It was all very well to draw arrows on charts to indicate the resupply of Allied invasion armies on the coastal littoral of a foreign country, but where and how the epic number of troops, munitions, supplies, trucks, and tanks would actually land was another matter entirely.

Amphibious assaults are a logistics and personnel challenge and the northern coast of France presented an especially difficult obstacle. Usable harbors were in enemy hands and heavily defended. Churchill had recognized the problem early on. His memo to Lord Mountbattan on May 30, 1942, "Piers for use on beaches," directs that "they must float up and down with [the] tide. The anchor problem must be mastered. Let me have the best solution worked out. Don't argue the matter. The difficulties will argue for themselves" (Professor Sir Alan Harris, "Mulberry Harbours," *Transactions of the Newcomen Society,* vol. 61, 1989–90). Later that summer, the calamitous raid on Dieppe further brought home the terrible reality of what a well-defended port can do against an attacking force. To succeed, Anglo-American planners needed to create harbors by artificial means, but how? The answer came from the Combined Chiefs of Staff who directed the prefabrication of artificial harbors, one American, one British, that would span all five invasion beaches: Utah, Omaha, Juno, Sword, and Gold. The overall code name tagged to the harbor project was Mulberry.

Creating the artificial harbors was a multiphased task, each with its own code name: Operation Corn Cob was the use of block ships that steamed or were towed across the channel and scuttled to form a breakwater, a steel mole of iron riprap. Gooseberry was the name given to the sheltered waters created by the sunken Corn Cob ships. Huge, armed breakwaters code-named Phoenix, together with piers and steel roadbeds inside the breakwaters, were built in secret in England and towed to France.

During the planning phase, the small cadre of officers who oversaw the details worked in London to be near their opposite numbers in the War Shipping Administration and the "hearty, ever-obliging Captain Jim Devlin, who was delighted at the thought of a combat role for his beloved cargo ships," noted Stanford (*Force Mulberry*). Men toiled around the clock to put the mobile harbors in place just offshore, within easy enemy gunnery range. Bofors 40-mm rapid-fire antiaircraft weapons were deployed on the Phoenixes. This was not much of a defense to be sure, but it gave the crews a feeling of confidence. The whole of the Overlord plan for the invasion pivoted on the success of the Mulberry harbors.

Later it was discovered that German intelligence mistook the floating behemoths for blocks to their seaports. Intelligence failures on this scale can decide the fate of nations. Captain A. Dayton Clark was the naval commander for Force Mulberry. In charge of Gooseberry One and Two was the New York–based naval architect and former volunteer RNVR lieutenant, now a newly appointed U.S. Navy lieutenant, George Hoague. With Hoague on the artificial harbor operation, as a liaison officer with the Royal Navy, was Charles Porter who had left the underground headquarters at the Nore and also transferred to the U.S. Navy.

"In organizing the blockship end of the breakwater, Operation Corn Cob," wrote Stanford, Lieutenant George Hoague "knew his business and charged forcefully into . . . dealing with the War Shipping Administration on crew problems, equipping the ships with extra antiaircraft armament, provisioning them and seeing that the scuttling charges were properly placed and wired. In fact his operation became so well organized that his group was used as a Siberia in the final days for ineffective officers who had proved to be unsuited in critical jobs. With Lieutenant Hoague, it was reasoned, they might be useful and could not prejudice the success of his undertaking" (*Force Mulberry*). On March 6 and 7, 1944, Phoenix progress received a substantial, if belated, forward step when the second towing trials revealed the sensational fact that one tug of 1,000 hp., not two as previously thought, could tow a Phoenix by using a new towing gear developed by the Portsmouth staff. A speed of three knots in calm water was attained.

By March 8 Lieutenant Hoague had twenty-six ships firmed for Mulberry allocation, "assuring 10,000 linear feet of breakwater against requirements of 9,000 ft." The ships were fitted with ballast, extra 20-mm AA guns, and explosive charges in their English port of discharge, and assembled in the northern ports of Oban and Methil. Thus the invasion was launched from ports and anchorages throughout Britain on June 6, 1944.

Hoague was credited with sending more U.S. ships to the bottom than anyone else, of either side. Journalists were fascinated with the Mulberry project. Hoague told reporters how American vessels—mostly beat-up cargo ships and one obsolete British warship—were filled with charges and taken across the English Channel to be lined up, anchored, and scuttled to make the breakwaters. Although resting on the bottom, their backs broken, the row of sunken ships held their place throughout the notorious gale of June 19–22, the worst storm in that region in eighty years. Not so fortunate were the concrete caissons paralleling the shore, many of which disintegrated on the third day. The storm wrecked United States' *Mulberry* and badly damaged the British one. They were cannibalized into one harbor at the British site.

Stanford was present throughout and gives a lively technical account of what occurred, as well as recording the interplay among the men who carried out this huge responsibility, literally and figuratively, under desperate conditions:

> At Omaha, during this first day (D+1), Captain Clark with Commander Passmore in HMCS *Gulnare* laid out the sites for the first six ships in Gooseberry II in the morning and marked the line with dan buoys. By noon, the first section of block ships arrived. Captain Clark threw his staff into consternation by boarding the block ship and relieving Lieutenant Hoague. Lieutenant Commander Bassett, Captain Clark announced, would sink the ship under his supervision. Lieutenant Hoague, who had followed every detail of the block ship fitting-out with such meticulous care and who had surmounted all obstacles so well, was thunderstruck. Lieutenant Commander Bassett was probably the most skilled ship and tug handler that could have been found anywhere. Nonetheless, it was a tough decision for Lieutenant Hoague to swallow.
>
> The merchant captain [of one of the Corn Cob ships] refused to participate and the crew was evacuated, whereupon Lieutenant Commander Bassett, great master with tugs that he was, sank the first block ship neatly and accurately. Lieutenant Hoague, admiring his skill, cheerfully joined him.

> Between 1500 and 2030 on June 7, three ships were sunk: the *James Iredell*, the *Baialoide,* and the *Galveston*. There had been little interruption from shore artillery fire until the last ship in this group went down. Then, shore batteries reached out and bracketed the ship. The Phoenix sinking teams that had been brought over by Commander Hunter-Blair in HMS *Minster* unfortunately had just been transferred to billets in the block ships to be ready for the arrival of the first Phoenix tows, awaited in the morning. Casualties due to shrapnel and shell fragments from this bombardment were inevitable.

The Mulberry team toiled around the clock knowing the survivors of the initial beach assaults, now clawing their way inland through Hitler's Atlantic Wall, were totally dependent on a rapid, sustained resupply. Failure meant being driven back into the sea, the invasion defeated. The success or otherwise of the Mulberry harbors would decide whether the Allied armies could prevail or be hammered to death, locked in place unable to maneuver, short of ammunition and provisions.

Merchant Marine historian Bruce Felknor wrote that Operation Mulberry began and continued under fire, and the most essential parts of the job, started on the evening of June 7, were completed on D+8, June 14, one day ahead of schedule. "It functioned so smoothly," Lester E. Ellison, first mate on a U.S. Army tug recalled, "that on June 14/18, an average of 8,500 tons of cargo poured ashore over it daily." They had exceeded the design quota of 5,000 tons by nearly 60 percent. After being unloaded the merchant ships returned to English ports for another cargo, some making three round-trips daily. This was during the height of the Buzz Bomb era, when the Straits of Dover area was known as "Doodlebug Alley" for the number of low-flying V-1 missiles overhead. HM *LST 198*, Konow's command, was among the ships that used the Mulberry to land troops and tanks.

The artificial harbors' early role was planned for the purpose of bringing stores and ammunition ashore, not landing personnel or vehicles. Necessity changed priorities and eventually the harbor on Gold Beach processed about a quarter of all British personnel put ashore in Normandy, continuing in service even after the major ports of Le Havre and Cherbourg had been liberated and opened to Allied traffic. By July 31 more than 627 million tons of supplies had been landed. Through these miraculous port facilities passed the men and machines of history's greatest amphibious operation: 156,000 troops with all their trucks and tanks and artillery pieces, along with all their food, fuel, and ammunition.

Supreme Commander of the Allied Expeditionary Force, General Eisenhower, applauded the success: "For the first time in history, a harbor has been built in sections, towed across the sea, and set down, during a battle, on the enemy shore" (*Force Mulberry*).

Hoague was injured the day after the great storm when he jumped off a pierhead onto one of the concrete pontoons and broke both heels. "It was really quite stupid of me," he said of the incident ("Yank Cited for Sinking U.S. Ships" *Seattle Post-Intelligencer,* 7 March 1945). For his extraordinary performance in making the critical project work during some of the most epic days in military annals, Hoague was awarded the Legion of Merit (with the "V" for valor device), an unusually senior American decoration rarely approved for anyone of such junior rank. Hoague was specifically cited for directing the creation of the two artificial harbors on schedule and without loss of life in the face of severe enemy resistance. France awarded him the Croix de Guerre.

When Ed Russell's daughter, Serena, was born at Blenheim Palace, the 10th Duke of Marlborough (Russell's father-in-law) sent his kinsman Winston Churchill, also born at Blenheim Palace, a dozen plover eggs. It was the gift of a splendid rarity on a wonderful occasion. After Russell transferred to the U.S. Navy he joined the staff for the planning of the Normandy invasion. His job was beachmaster with an engineering brigade that hit Omaha Beach on the morning of June 6. Beachmasters controlled Allied traffic directly under the gun sights of the defending German army.

Years later Russell reminisced,

> I may not recognize the president of our largest account, nor remember with whom I lunched last Tuesday, but I recall every heartbeat of June 5 and 6, and a ridiculous amount of detail before and after those stirring days. So, I am sure, do thousands of those who crossed Omaha Beach on D-Day. Summer days are long in England and though the weather was foul, daylight lasted well after 10:00 P.M. on June 5. I was one of the last

to board USS *Ancon* lying under Portland Bill. *Ancon* was the flagship of Rear Admiral Hall, another of whose flagships had transported me to Operation Husky, the Sicilian invasion. (Serena Balfour papers)

Russell continued,

> At such times the dramatic seems almost called for, and while waiting to embark, I scribbled a last letter. As the boat came alongside, I scooped up a handful of England, which suddenly was "home." A photograph of my wife and three-month-old daughter was pasted in my helmet. I attached sinister significance to its loss later as I scrambled down a cargo net to the landing craft. This was it! Battleships and cruisers opened fire, anchor chains rattled and boat davits creaked with the steel decks clanking to soldiers' boots. Five thousand vessels, 6,500 aircraft, a half-million men and more fire-power than ever before mustered were going to grab a foothold on the European continent. (ibid.)

The overwhelming amount of minutiae that attached itself to efforts of this magnitude staggered the mind:

Allowances had to be made but timing precise; underwater demolition teams had to clear and buoy channels; beachmasters had to have their designated flags in place shortly after H-hour;

The tide rose 23 feet in the morning and 22 feet in the afternoon on D-day. There was 2,500 feet between high- and low-water marks which meant the tide came in at about 1 foot per minute;

Force I comprising 34,000 men and 3,300 vehicles would be landed on Omaha in the forenoon and Force B with 25,000 men and 4,400 vehicles began landing in early afternoon. An additional force of 17,000 men and 2,300 vehicles waited in the transport area to come ashore.

Russell remembered,

> We had planned carefully and well and were more than a match for the enemy, and even for the unpleasant surprise of a first-line [Wehrmacht]

> division where we expected static troops. But no one can plan on the weather. The storm that churned the [English] Channel was unequalled. The 24-hour postponement meant seasick men cramped in airless compartments for days. All major elements arrived off the beach on schedule, but the rough seas made the launching and loading of assault craft most difficult. The foul weather reduced visibility and the frightening number and variety of craft confused coxswains.
>
> From the boat we waded 50 yards to the muddy sand and flopped as a shell whined out to sea. I lay face down, wet, sick, shaking with cold and scared, very scared. Not only did I assume that we on the beach were done-for, I was terrified for my family and all behind. [But] as confusion had bred confusion, action began to inspire action. In spite of small-arms fire, men began moving mechanically to untangle the mess.
>
> It was my job to help coordinate Naval Beachmaster activities with the Army's Special Engineer brigade. We were supposed to control traffic and organize the flow of men and supplies over the beach. The only other gear I carried ashore was a blanket and a small bottle of port. I buried these in a half dug foxhole. (Hours later, when I could have used both, I found someone else wrapped in my blanket and the empty bottle nearby.) Many boats "grounded" on sandbars and discharged their passengers in deep water. GIs died without firing a shot. Few vehicles were operable and on a rising tide were quickly submerged. The enemy was still dug-in just above the beach. Five hundred bombers were to have dropped thousands of tons of bombs on those defenses, but because of the weather the bombardment missed by as much as three miles.
>
> The tide began to fall and most of the grass fires burned out, exposing even more chaos. The falling water exposed wrecked jeeps, trucks, bulldozers and artillery. Tanks, with their crews tragically drowned inside and with their tattered flotation gear looking like shrouds, rose from the deep. (ibid.)

He concludes, "I have always been squeamish about anything dead and was shocked at my indifference to the many bodies lying amongst the collective junk at the high-water mark. I can only remember how very peaceful and lifelike they all appeared, and what a shame and waste." His brave conduct during the invasion earned him the award of the Bronze Star Medal. The citation describes how Russell landed on the beach on the early morning of June 6 and remained there continuously for twenty-three days successfully coordinating the beach organization.

During various phases of the Normandy invasion, Cherry served on HMS *Riou* and HMS *Wren* of the famous Captain F. J. Walker's 2nd Support Group, which held the record for sinking U-boats in the Battle of the Atlantic. Gibson participated in the greatest amphibious invasion in history aboard HMS *Tyler*, tasked on D-day with escorting British Merchant Navy Bibby Line troop ships to the British sector beachheads of Sword and Juno. Two hours after H-hour the ships began to supply urgently needed reinforcements. Later, Gibson convoyed channel steamers carrying troops to the northern area of the invasion site. Jim Bacon was a rating aboard *Tyler*. "Following training," he said,

> I qualified as a Telegraphist and joined an American-built destroyer escort, HMS *Tyler*, in April 1944. We were soon involved escorting merchant ships in the Battle of the Atlantic. It was a horrifying spectacle to one minute seeing a ship in sight and then an almighty explosion as, hit by a torpedo, the ship would become an exploding wreck, particularly if it was carrying oil or ammunition. HMS *Tyler* was eventually transferred to assist the final preparation for the D-Day landings, escorting troop ships and landing craft to the beaches and then back with casualties. When the beaches were established we patrolled the area against any German U-boats or aircraft or torpedo boats attempting to attack the supply craft. (S.V. C. Cambridge, "Memoirs of a Typical Teenager," BBC, *WW2 People's War*, 27 May 2005)

HMS *Tyler* was briefly anchored near HMS *Belfast*, a cruiser, which was firing "continuous salvoes of 4-inch shells to targets behind the beaches, causing havoc to German troops and supplies."

Edmund Kittredge was also part of Operation Neptune, the naval annex to Operation Overlord. He was among the commandos who went ashore in the first assault wave to determine whether landing craft, or subsequent troop assaults, could follow the same track. Training made the commandos very effective at dealing with the Germans, a task they found actually less difficult than dealing with the congestion on the beaches. Just as Russell had observed, wrecked boats and vehicles were a major problem especially when the vehicles blocked exits inland from the beachhead. Despite great difficulties the teams managed to clear obstacles, organize the routes, and bring supplies ashore. Kittredge and his commandos stayed on the beaches for about six weeks helping in a variety of unglamorous chores like salvaging sunken landing craft and mooring Mulberry harbors. He stayed at Juno through late August, retrieving corpses in the surf line. "If corpses are washed up on the beach," directed Juno Headquarters, "it is the responsibility of the Beach Party to remove the corpse from the water to above the high water mark." The directive added, "If the body is identified as a Naval rating it will be dealt with by the Royal Navy" ("Disposal of Corpses," Memorandum No. 28, N.O.I.C. Juno Headquarters, 28 August 1944, Kittredge family papers).

In early summer 1944, Konow's HM *LST 198* staged at Harwich, England, in company with thirty other LSTs embarking tanks and troops for the invasion. Their next stop was an area south of the Isle of Wight, nicknamed "Piccadilly Circus," where an armada of warships of every description assembled to await the attack order and from where all sea-lanes went straight to the Normandy coast. HM *LST 198* followed her channel markers to a lightship with the code name of "target beach." Konow participated in the most spectacular amphibious operation in maritime history.

LST 198 headed for Sword. After delivering his cargo of tanks and troops Konow returned with captured German soldiers. They took one thousand prisoners of war from France to Portsmouth on the first day of the invasion. Konow thought the soldiers looked shell-shocked. Earlier, in the Italian campaign when *LST 198* took aboard a mix of German and Italian troops the intra-Axis relationship was tense and violent. He reported it was more difficult to prevent the POWs from killing each other than it was to protect the crew from the POWs. The Germans despised the Italians and the Italians were terrified of the Germans. After the first bad experience, Konow never again took aboard groups of German and Italian soldiers together. Other ships did the same. Shortly after D-day Konow became commanding officer of HM *LST 198* and from June 1944 until the end of the war he moved wherever Allied forces needed him.

HMT *Prince Leopold* met her fate on July 29, 1944. Part of Force J for the Normandy landings, she was torpedoed and sunk by *U-621*, which was itself sunk with all hands by two Canadian destroyers, HMCS *Ottawa* and HMCS *Chaudiere*.

To help make the lights go on again all over the world, the fifty-mile-wide stretch of the Normandy amphibious landings and the savage hedgerow country fighting in the weeks that followed cost more than 209,000 Allied casualties, including wounded and missing in action. Nearly 37,000 ground forces died and 16,714 Allied Air Force personnel were killed. The 21st Army Group (British, Canadian, and Polish ground forces) suffered more than 83,000 casualties; U.S. ground troop casualties numbered nearly 126,000. Between 15,000 and 20,000 French civilians died. Without Operation Mulberry the cost would have been unimaginably higher.

As the rest of the war ground on, nearing its end, the volunteers moved with the flow. By 1945 Kittredge was in Singapore waiting for the Allied invasion of Japan. For the rest of his life he kept a copy of what might have been written by an Australian army private in pencil on the wall of a Japanese prison cell on an offshore island:

Last Post

If I must face the firing squad
Tho' harm I did no body,
Teach him to love them still my God
As bullets strike my body.

If I must die a lonely spy
Tho' spying did I never,
Stay in my heart, Oh God, and I
Will love them more than ever.

Forgive them all the tortures done
My thirst and long starvation,
For who could suffer more than one
Who died for our salvation.

Pte I. M. Nick 13th Dec. '42

Kittredge also copied from the same wall and written by the same soldier: "4 nights and 3 days without food or water. Nick Dec 42. Dec 10, 11, 12, 13, 14, 15, 16, 17 off to CHANGI. No food, Nick." Changi was a Japanese-run prisoner-of-war camp.

Henry Clark, a petty officer who served with Kittredge, recalled, "I have a clear picture of him in my mind. Even after sixty years. I do remember that the other POs and I were broke so we asked him to lend us ten shillings to go to the village pub for a drink. Beer was one shilling a pint. Mr. Kittredge said borrowing was against King's Regulations and Admiralty Instructions but if the Beach Master would agree then he would lend us it. The Beach Master was an officer in the regular Royal Navy and when we asked him, he said 'Yes, and ask him to lend me ten bob.' " Clark remembered also that Kittredge "gave a talk on how we had to build up the country after the war. I got the impression he had conservative views. He pointed out that if we elected a Labour Government we would have most industries nationalized. I thought after the war how he must have been disappointed. Labour romped in" (Harry Howlett letter to R. E. White, 5 August 2001, Charlotte Hammond collection).

Homans shipped out to the war in the Pacific in a U.S. Navy uniform. "I joined USS *Stringham* (APD-6), a high-speed transport, in Guam," he wrote,

> at about 11:45 one morning and was sitting in the cabin of one of the officers waiting for the captain and other officers to get through lunch so that I could introduce myself, when I heard a crash. At first, I thought that a kamikaze had gotten way off course, but I rushed up on deck and discovered that USS *Lavalette* (DD 448), being in hand steering, having been seriously damaged in Okinawa, had attempted to come alongside to moor but went forward instead of going back and rammed us. The damage control officer saw me on deck and said, "You relieve me." He then left and I spent about five hours in my beautifully clean and pressed khakis supervising the plugging of the hole in the ship's side. When I went on deck and reported to the captain that she was not going to sink, there was a great groan from the crew.

Lieutenant Commander Ed Russell, USNR, finished the war aboard the cruiser USS *Oklahoma City*, also in the Pacific.

In summer 1944, commanding an underwater demolition team, Draper Kauffman led his men in a daylight reconnaissance thirty yards from fortified enemy beaches on the island of Saipan. Under heavy gunfire the team carried out a successful survey of the beaches and its approaches to identify and destroy obstacles that could endanger the landings. A month later Kauffman led Underwater Team 5 in night reconnaissance of the heavily defended landing beaches on the island of Tinian. After recovering the reconnaissance team it was discovered there was a man missing. Kauffman, who had already swum the four miles to the beach and back, returned to the reef two miles away under enemy fire to search for the missing sailor. This was the first-ever daylight reconnaissance of a hostile beach, and it occurred with an entire invasion fleet riding the swells with nothing to do but watch and monitor the commando team's radio communications. For his actions that day Kauffman was awarded a second Navy Cross.

Thousands of miles away in the other direction, the war in Europe was ending. Alex Cherry applied for transfer to the U.S. Navy. He wrote, "With the German war drawing to a close, circumstances called for a review of my own situation. Only in the Pacific was the war still being determined by naval action. And there I now wanted to be with my own people." The Royal Navy approved the request and put him on an indefinite leave pending his departure to U.S. forces. Cherry was interviewed at the U.S. Navy's Grosvenor Square headquarters. He waited. "I lived in a sort of vacuum, neither a part of the Royal Navy nor the U.S. Navy. And if I was refused by the U.S. Navy the war for me would be over" (*Yankee RN*).

Two months passed before he was told that the U.S. quota of naval officers was full, and his application denied. "I couldn't believe it," he mourned. Fortunately, the Admiralty took him back at once. With unusual creativity for a military bureaucracy, he got an assignment particularly well suited to his talents. Cherry was promoted to commander and sent to a shore billet in HMS *Royal Katherine*—the Royal Navy's headquarters in occupied Germany. As British Naval Liaison Officer, Bremen, he performed with exceptional skill. Rear Admiral Hutton, (British) Flag Officer, Western Germany, wrote that Cherry "has conducted himself to my entire satisfaction. A keen and capable officer whose loyalty and common sense have made him an excellent liaison officer." The commander of U.S. Naval Forces in Germany cited Cherry for "Exceptional meritorious performance of duty" (A. G. Robinson, Commander, U.S. Ports & Bases, Germany, Letter of Appreciation to Commander Cherry, File No. P15, Serial 1826, U.S. Ports & Bases, Germany, 10 November 1945). In the early 1950s, around the time of the Korean War, Cherry was disappointed again in a second attempt to obtain a commission in the U.S. Navy. Physicians and chaplains may get a waiver to come in at a senior rank but commander is not an entry-level rank for line officers.

There is a popular misconception that occupation of an enemy country is only a new dimension for the fighting forces; having fired the last shot, they take over the governing functions. In fact, control of post–Third Reich Germany fell to a vast contingent of uniformed and civilian personnel with the military and political skills to work out the intent and purpose of what was to be achieved, and to define the means and methods. The issue now was not winning the war but winning the peace that would confront the Allies upon the collapse and surrender of Germany.

Cherry became part of an elite cadre of staff officers who were schooled in the objectives of the Occupation. His part of the mission focused on the demobilization of the German fleet and naval fortifications and problems with shipyards and docks. There were issues relating to the shipping necessary to sustain the Army of Occupation, and the need to ferret out technical data that might be useful in the war against Japan that was still raging. Also, Germany's harbors and rivers had to be cleared of mines. Cherry did his job well; so much so that he was appointed an Officer of the Most Excellent Order of the British Empire (Military Division) in the King's Birthday Honours List of 1946.

When it came, the German army's collapse was sudden. Ports started to fall in very rapid succession. All available transportation was diverted to get the British army into Germany as quickly as possible. David Gibson was assigned to 21st Army Group (Field Marshall Montgomery's command in Northwest Europe), with the job of naval liaison officer at Q Movements. Gibson said this meant "begging and pleading" for transport to move naval personnel from one liberated port to the next. His former ship, HMS *Tyler*, was assigned the job of collecting surrendered U-boats. Roy Emmington and six other torpedomen from her crew became a boarding party armed with revolvers and 9-mm Sten guns. "I didn't think it was a good idea [to have] torpedo men with guns and loaded with live ammunition but we managed to bring over a number of

U-boats without any accidents," he wrote. One trip was different. "I was on the conning tower with the captain of the U-boat when he asked me, 'is that your Frigate over there?' I said 'Yes.' He went on, 'We have been closer than this.' It turned out that a few months before the war ended we were steaming out of Pembroke Dock and we hit what we thought was a log and it took our Asdic Dome off. The U-boat Captain told me we had run him down and took his periscope off. I mentioned it to Captain Rankin [*Tyler*'s skipper] and he invited the U-boat captain onboard for dinner." In a reflective tone Emmington remarked on the enemy he had faced for so many years and with whom he had to work immediately following the war. "People used to ask me how we got on with German sailors," he wrote. "Not many could speak English but those who could said they would never have given in" (Roy Emmington letter, "History of HMS *Tyler*," www.navsource.org/archives/06/567).

V-E day caught Cherry at Tilbury Docks, down the Thames, just as he was preparing to leave with his convoy of specialists to take over German ports. "Ships in harbour were flying every bit of color they could muster," he wrote. "The air tingled with excitement, of mounting gaiety. The British Isles . . . was in the throes of victory and a Continent was in the throes of emancipation . . . all the whistles, sirens, and foghorns in the area let go with a prolonged blast that stifled conversation for an hour" (*Yankee RN*).

EPILOGUE

Upwards of 5,000 ships and 60,000 men died in the Battle of the Atlantic. Today, luxury cruise ships steam unaware over ground made sacred by a terrible sacrifice. Far below their keels lie fingers that once grasped lines, gripped a helm, or gently tapped on a glass engine gauge. Among the undulating sands of the seabed the bones of men are scattered in ships torn apart by the violent actions of other men. Vertebrae that bent against winter gales mingle in the tangled wiring of silent communications systems. Shattered bulkheads seal passageways where U-boat torpedoes let loose their fury, rupturing equally the steel plates of a warship or cargo-laden merchantman. Letters waiting to be posted at the arrival port rotted to nothing. Seabags and duffels stashed in lockers to be hurriedly packed for the next shore leave and home have disintegrated. Bows that once had a "bone in their teeth" are marine habitats in the unrelieved blackness of the deep. The only sign of what lies below may be oil seepage that might still escape from bunkers. The casual human eye is unlikely to note their flecks on the surface.

London has been repaired though unexploded Luftwaffe bombs still turn up here and there to remind us of Kauffman's work, Taylor taking to the air to intercept the enemy, and Hayes tending to broken bodies in the Blitz. Dead soldiers rest in ordered rows on the Normandy coast where they breached Hitler's Fortress Europe. Russell would be hard-pressed today to find where he had worked on D-day, or Kittredge where it was that he hauled to dry sand the dead who rolled up in the surf line. Jungle has long since covered the Japanese emplacements that menaced Lee and Leggat, and the wall on which a starved

Allied soldier wrote his own epitaph. Cherry's German occupation ports are brisk centers of commerce. Japan is a wealthy democracy.

Gone for the most part from the American scene is the patrician nobility that made volunteering for a greater good such a natural act. Centered in New England, but found throughout the United States in the early years of the twentieth century, was a class of men and women who freely stepped forward when the need arose. They considered service to be a duty. The preppie establishment that produced the likes of Morison, the Parkers, Gibson, Porter, Homans, Hayes, Kittredge, and the others has vanished almost as totally as the popular ukulele Cherry carried with him when he went to war. The Ivy League schools the men attended are today indifferent, even hostile, to the scholar-soldier principle of service above self. Ever since the Vietnam War, Harvard refuses to allow a campus-based Reserve Officer Training Corps. The tradition that bound old money and venerable institutions with obligations of citizenship is now the relic of a bygone era.

Most of the men of the World War II generation have passed over the horizon, friend and foe alike. Ed Russell was the only surviving RNVR volunteer to attend the Greenwich rededication ceremony. David Gibson was the last survivor. We owe them witness. By our continued ability to remember their words and deeds we pass along the epic story of their willing hearts and brave conduct. We mark the places where they have passed and we tell their story.

> When You Go Home, Tell Them Of Us And Say,
> For Their Tomorrow, We Gave Our Today.
>
> *John Maxwell Edmonds (1875–1958)*

American volunteers for the Royal Naval Volunteer Reserve in the order of their commissioning dates:

William Erwin Gibson Taylor, September 14, 1939
David Arnold van Epps, September 2, 1940
Draper Laurence Kauffman, September 27, 1940
Oswald Birrell Deiter, March 24, 1941
Derek Armitage Lee, April 10, 1941

*Edward Mortimer Ferris, May 19, 1941
*John Stanley Parker, June 7, 1941
*Charles Burnham Porter, June 19, 1941
Gurdan Buck, June 19, 1941
John Matthew Leggat, July 14, 1941
Alex Henry Cherry, July 19, 1941
Edmund Webster Kittredge, August 14, 1941
Carl Frederik Sophus Vilhelm Konow, August 23, 1941
George Hoague Jr., August 23, 1941
David Gibson, August 23, 1941
John Albert Stilwell, September 8, 1941
Henry Fremont Ripley, September 8, 1941
Edwin Fairman Russell, October 1, 1941
John Edward Hampson, October 6, 1941
Francis Mason Hayes, October 17, 1941
William Perkins Homans, October 21, 1941
Peter Greene Morison, November 10, 1941

*"The First Three" indicated by the plaque in the Painted Hall, Royal Naval College, Greenwich.

APPENDIX I

Reflections by *Kapitän zur See* Otto von Bülow

In autumn 1942 my command, *U-404*, attacked east-bound RB-1, a convoy of escorted river steamers in mid-Atlantic, west of Ireland. On September 25, 1942, I sank the ships *New York* and *Boston*. The next morning I sank HMS *Veteran*. The loss of life was great, for not only did the destroyer's officers and crew of 159 perish but also among the lost were the 78 men from *New York* and *Boston* who had been rescued from the sea by HMS *Veteran* the day before.

I commissioned *U-404* in Danzig in August 1941. After shake-down training in the Baltic Sea we departed from Kiel on the first war patrol. Then and in five following war patrols in the North Atlantic and on the East Coast of the United States till July 1943 we spent over 270 days at sea. In that time we sank 14 Allied ships. My fate and that of HMS *Veteran* began to converge on August 23 when we left our home port of St. Nazaire. When RB-1 came into the picture we had been stopped with diesel engine problems, and hurried to join the attack. There were fog banks that morning and a heavy swell in very light air. Visibility was intermittent. At 0925 we sighted a big steamer heading southwest and followed at full speed. Eleven minutes later our lookout reported a destroyer to starboard, behind the beam, following the steamer.

I dived almost immediately to attack the destroyer but lost contact by periscope due to the heavy swell and poor visibility. At 1012 I surfaced and sighted two big freighters to starboard ahead of the beam and dived to prepare a three-torpedo spread against the target. At 1035 all of a sudden a destroyer appeared in the periscope, straight ahead at a distance of seven hundred meters and at an angle of 90 degrees, going slowly. Due to the new situation [a warship within range, instead of the convoy] the angle of the torpedo spread was narrowed and at 1036 I fired the three-torpedo spread. About a minute later after, respectively, 53 seconds and 57 seconds, two detonations are heard confirming hits. I then dived to a depth of one hundred meters to escape pursuit.

U-404 in my time had a crew of 45 plus a *Kriegsberichterstatter-film* who came aboard to shoot motion picture footage of life aboard an *Unterseeboot*. The film survives, amazingly. The sea battle in the waters between the United States and Europe pivoted on the U-boat war and the loss of life, ships, and material was epic on both sides. *Oberleutnant* Adolf Schönberg relieved me on July 19. Nine days later he was dead when *U-404* was lost with all hands in the Bay of Biscay, sunk by American and British Liberator aircraft. For 1942, the U-boat service lost 86 boats. The following year the loss was 243 boats. The submarine kill rate among all combatants on both sides of the conflict was heavy, but German losses are in a class by themselves. By the time the war ended over 700 boats were lost in combat, out of 1,162 boats commissioned. U-boats in World War II sank 175 warships and 2,603 merchant ships accounting for the death of 30,246 Allied merchant seamen. Over 27,491 U-boat crew (of about 39,000 who joined) perished with them.

I was blessed. I survived and had the privilege to grow very old. When the war was over I came home from POW captivity and in time joined the new Federal German Navy—the *Bundesmarine*. In 1960 I commissioned my second command, the blandly named destroyer *Z-6*: ex–USS *Charles Ausburne* (DD 570) formerly the flagship of Captain (later, Admiral) Arleigh "31-Knot" Burke's Little Beaver Squadron. I retired in the rank of *Kapitän zur See* in 1970. By growing as old as I have, I lived to see another dictatorship topple, that of the Soviet Union, and the reunification of my broken country. Great age also brings with it time to reflect on the past, to think about old battles and the slaughter of men I have known and loved, and those whom I never knew but whom fate made my enemies for a time. I think about them all.

I have prayed for the fallen sailors with whom I served and against whom I fought, and I hope they pray for me. In the spirit of reconciliation and in memory of the fearful losses suffered by the navies of both sides, and most particularly for the men and ships described in these pages, thank you for giving me the opportunity to contribute to the making of this book and of the story it tells.

—Otto von Bülow

Otto v. Bülow died in Aumühle on January 5, 2006, aged 94 years.

APPENDIX II

Biographical Notes

Gurdan Buck. Born January 27, 1906, in Niagara Falls, New York. Raised in a Maryland farming family, Buck was educated at a preparatory school and Cambridge University, England. When the Royal Navy released him he at once enlisted in the U.S. Navy as a boatswain's mate second class. In July 1942 Buck was commissioned as a lieutenant (junior grade), USNR, and assigned to Boston. His last duty station was with the Amphibious Force, Little Creek in Norfolk, Virginia. Buck's military tenure as a naval officer in Britain and the United States ended almost certainly because he could not break free of the winery vault. England let him go scarcely three months after his commissioning and never informed the U.S. Navy. U.S. military records list a general court-martial on July 9, 1942, and dismissal from the service on October 30, 1942. In fairness to Buck, before the 1948 reforms leading to the Uniform Code of Military Justice, naval jurisprudence could be of the rough and crude "deck plate" variety, only marginally better than the capricious "rocks and shoals" of the eighteenth and early nineteenth century. In World War II heavy smoking and drinking were tolerated with patient bemusement; it was also how people dealt with soul-destroying tension. A latter-day scold on tobacco and alcohol does not understand a world war. Buck died on October 24, 1991.

Alex Henry Cherry. Born June 11, 1901, in New York City. His parents were naturalized U.S. citizens who had emigrated from Latvia to the United States, but his mother was born of British parents. Cherry stayed in the Royal Navy throughout the war. Following his return to civilian life on January

26, 1947, he was employed briefly as a senior-level staffer in federal government service in occupied Germany. He then returned to New York City and resumed his career with a brokerage and in real estate investments; he was quite successful. Cherry became an active member of the New York Commandery of the Naval Order of the United States, a membership-by-invitation-only organization and the country's oldest military fraternal group. Although acceptance at that time was restricted to commissioned officers of the U.S. Navy, Marine Corps, and Coast Guard, Cherry's British service was welcomed. He was the order's historian general and also a life member of the order's parent organization, the U.S. Navy League. Cherry gained a measure of fame with the successful publication of his memoirs in 1951; *Yankee RN* went through seven editions. He had one son, Richard, now deceased, who said he never learned the identity of his mother. In a single note found in a lot of Cherry's personal papers sold at auction after his death, the name Rosalind Holden appears in the block on a form that asked for his wife's name. Alex Cherry died in Florida on April 2, 1987.

HM assignments: *Malaya*, *Nimrod*, *Reading*, *Osprey*, *Caldwell*, *Whitehall*, *Riou* (first lieutenant), *Evadne*, *Wren* (first lieutenant), *Braithwaite*, *President,* Chatham Gunnery School, and *Royal Katherine.*

Heyward Cutting. The American volunteer in the British Army, who had been a guest of Ambassador Winant at the U.S. Embassy, went home and finished his education on the GI Bill at Harvard.

Oswald Birrell Deiter. Born November 15, 1903, in Dansville, New York. He passed up the opportunity to transfer to U.S. forces and stayed in the Royal Navy. Deiter and Ellaline Macey divorced after the war. He returned to the United States where he married his high school sweetheart. They had two children. The family settled in Ridgewood, New Jersey, where Deiter opened a practice. After more than twenty years living abroad, he had come back to live not far from the place where he spent much of his youth. In Ridgewood he was chairman of the Civil Defense Committee, president of the Joe Jefferson Club, a member of the West Side Presbyterian Church, and an active fisherman. Oswald Birrell Deiter died on July 20, 1979.

HM assignments: HMML *115*, which he also commanded, *Nimrod,* and *Seahawk.*

Edward Mortimer Ferris. In London he met and married Kathleen Parry. A daughter, Henrietta, nicknamed Penni, was born on August 14, 1944. Promoted to commander (Cherry was the other volunteer to attain senior officer rank in the Royal Navy), his last assignment was Senior British Officer West Coast, San Francisco. He died in New York City on August 17, 1983.

HM assignments: *La Melpomene*, *Sennen*, and *Byard,* which he commanded.

David Gibson. Born September 19, 1919, in Pittsburgh, Pennsylvania. Gibson remained in the Royal Navy throughout the war and into the immediate postwar period, helping to return some of the U.S. Lend-Lease ships. It was not until the end of 1946 that he took his discharge and returned to civilian life. He re-enrolled at Yale and graduated in 1947, majoring in English language and literature. David Gibson died on January 18, 2002, in Washington, D.C.

HM assignments: *Burnham*, *Badger*, *Gardiner*, *Willowherb*, *Tyler,* and *Saker.*

John Edward Hampson. Born September 20, 1907, in Bardsdale, California, where his father ranched on the edge of Los Padres National Forest, Ventura County. Like some of the others who came to volunteer for England, Hampson's age and lack of experience thwarted any hope of acceptance by a U.S. military that functioned almost to the eve of war on a peacetime mindset when it came to selecting personnel. No other information was discovered to illuminate the details of his life in the Royal Navy, or what he did in later years. Hampson died in February 1983, in Los Angeles, California. Alcoholism is listed as a cause of death.

HM assignments: 780 Squadron, *Landrail*, 772 Squadron, *Goshawk*, 750 Squadron (?).

Francis Mason Hayes. Born September 14, 1912, in Pelham Manor, New York. Hayes was the first-born and only son of Frank Anderson Hayes and Effie Huntington. He went to London with his inventor father to discuss a patent for an automatic transmission and there met his future wife, Georgette Anderson. She was the daughter of the lawyer who represented the patent's use in England and she had accompanied her father to meet the visiting Americans. Smitten, Frankie transferred from Yale to Gonville and Caius College, Cambridge University, to complete his medical studies. He married Georgette in 1936. Their son, John Peter Hayes, was born in September 1937. It was John who, so many years later at the ceremony in Painted Hall, laid a wreath in memory of his father, HMS *Veteran,* and her crew. Hayes received his practical training at Guy's Hospital, in London. He was commissioned on the anniversary of the day in 1932 when he first registered as a surgeon at Guys; it was also on the day John Parker was killed. Frankie's accomplishments include membership in the Royal College of Surgeons. When Hayes entered the Navy his wife joined the American Red Cross. During the first part of the Blitz Hayes served as the deputy resident surgeon on full-time emergency duty at Guys and then was appointed resident surgeon in charge of Miller General Hospital in Greenwich. He entered the RNVR at HMS *Pembroke*, Chatham Naval Base. Georgette Hayes remarried in 1948 when John was eleven years old. John gave up his British citizenship (he was a dual national) and made his life in the United States. He raises horses in Maryland.

HM assignments: *Pembroke*, *Veteran*.

George Hoague Jr. Born August 30, 1904, in Brookline, Massachusetts. Hoague's injury to his heels at Normandy was severe. He was medically discharged from the U.S. Navy at St. Albans Naval Hospital, New York, in August 1946. He married Irene Hardy, a Women's Royal Naval Service officer serving at Caxton Hall, London. In World War II Caxton Hall was used by the Ministry of Information as a venue for press conferences held by Winston Churchill and his ministers. The couple had two children, a boy and a girl. Hoague became a diplomat with the United Nations. He and Irene lived in Switzerland and Majorca, rented a mansion in England, skied in the Alps, and even built their own yacht (in Spain, for $25,000—a princely sum in its day), and chartered voyages from New York to St. Thomas, Virgin Islands.

In late 1956 Hoague captained a wooden-hulled yacht from Miami to the Virgin Islands. The boat sprang a bad leak during hurricane-force winds that snapped the mast in two and ripped away a large section of the hull planking. Immensely energetic patching inside the hull and outside, and constant bailing were demanded of the captain and his small crew to save the boat and all aboard. The physical effort overwhelmed him and on January 24, 1957, George Hoague died at sea of exhaustion and exposure. His remains were committed to the deep four hundred miles northeast of Bermuda on the same day. His son, George, wrote "I was only ten when he lost his life. Although it has been over fifty years, I can still remember [that] my father's life was the sea, and every chance he got he found himself sailing. Our rescue came via the flying fish fishing boats who arranged for the Coast Guard to come and tow us back to Barbados. That was quite an experience for me and I will never forget the control my father had during this trying ordeal" (correspondence to authors).

Historical note: Hoague had crossed the Atlantic aboard RMS *Laconia,* newly refitted in St. John's. About some ships and the stories that attach themselves to their fate, exactly a year to the day after Hoague was aboard for the voyage to England, the RMS *Laconia* was torpedoed by *U-156* (*Kapitänleutnant* Werner Hartenstein). Her passengers included 1,800 Italian POWs, 80 civilians, 268 military personnel, and the 160 Polish soldiers who guarded the POWs, plus 136 ship's crew. *U-156* surfaced and when Hartenstein grasped the enormity of the human toll struggling in the water around him he ordered a rescue effort. Survivors accommodated aboard his U-boat numbered 200, and 200 people went into lifeboats. Hartenstein sent an open, uncoded message offering not to attack anyone who came to assist and, via encrypted message, also asked for assistance from any other Axis submarine in the vicinity. *Kapitänleutnant* Erich Würdemann arrived to help. A few hours later *U-507* (*Korvettenkapitän* Harro Schacht) and the Italian submarine *Cappellini* (Commander Salvatore Todaro) arrived. The small fleet of submarines draped with Red Cross flags headed for shore, towing a string of lifeboats.

Late on the morning of September 16, an American B-24 Liberator bomber from Ascension came upon the extraordinary scene and radioed for instructions. It was ordered to attack immediately. The submarines were forced to cut their lines to the lifeboats and dive. Hundreds of people again found themselves struggling in the open ocean. By luck, Vichy French warships arrived on scene and picked up survivors. Roughly 1,500 survived the sinking, including those taken aboard U-boats. The incident prompted Grand Admiral Dönitz to issue the "*Laconia* order" instructing his submarine commanders not to engage in rescue operations of any kind. Dönitz's order was sharply criticized. The "*Laconia* order" was used as evidence to convict him at the Nuremberg War Crimes trials. *U-156* was sunk on March 8, 1943, east of Barbados, with the loss of all hands. The Dönitz order was frequently ignored by his submarine commanders: Hans-Georg Hess on *U-995* fished out two young Russian sailors from winter waters near Murmansk.

HM assignments: *Laconia, Ausonia. Sennen.*

William Perkins Homans. Born March 18, 1921, in Boston, Massachusetts. On March 7, 1943, while serving aboard HMS *Ironbound*, Homans transferred to the U.S. Navy in the rank of ensign, his hard-gained Royal Navy experience completely ignored. In a letter to a former shipmate, Homans wrote, "The reason I appeared to be the most seaworthy—knowledgeable officer was what you may never have known. In October 1941, being upset that we were not in the war I joined the British Navy, where I was a lieutenant having a good deal of experience handling small ships until March 1943, when I transferred to the USN. I lost all my seniority about which I was quite resentful." Homans added with good humor that "I finished my great Navy career (except for the submarine reserves which I later joined) as garbage supervision officer on the docks in Boston. Good for a cup of coffee at each ship I visited and duty over by 1015" (6 November 1995, letter to Bill List, USS *Dextrous* reunion, Linthicum, Maryland, Peter Homans collection). He left the U.S. Naval Reserve in 1960 with the rank of lieutenant commander.

He graduated from Harvard Law School in 1948 and specialized in criminal law, especially civil liberties issues, throwing himself into his work and never charging enough for his skill and commitment, standing for the underdog for his entire life. Homans was a brilliant, driven attorney who did not press his clients for payment and was often obliged to seek out friends for help in financial crises. He possessed a brilliant legal mind. A U.S. federal superior court judge complimented him for a defense "as principled and tenacious and acute as any I have seen" (Edgar J. Bellefontaine, "'Enigmatic Giant' Was Hero to Attorneys," *Massachusetts Lawyers Weekly*, 6 June 1997). His arguments led the Massachusetts Supreme Judicial Court to abolish the death penalty in 1975. Homans is described as being an imposing figure who spoke in a rich, booming baritone, giving special emphasis to Aaron Burr's dictum that "the law is whatever is boldly asserted and plausibly maintained." His two marriages ended in divorce. William Perkins Homans Jr. died at the age of seventy-five on February 7, 1997 (Mark S. Brodin, *William P. Homans Jr: A Life in Court,* Florida:Vandeplas, 2010).

HM ships served on: *Ironbound*, *Tamarine*, *Duncton*.

Draper Laurence Kauffman. Born August 4, 1911, on Coronado Island, just offshore the southern California city of San Diego. Kauffman's commanding officer nominated him for the Medal of Honor for an act of extraordinary personal bravery in the face of the enemy. The recommendation was endorsed throughout the fleet's chain of command and sent to the regional commander for approval. By the time the paperwork arrived, a man had reduced the award to a Navy Cross before forwarding it to the Pentagon for final action: Kauffman's father. The elder Kauffman said he simply could not endorse his own son for the Medal of Honor, recalls his grandson, Draper Kauffman Jr. To do so would have invited whispers of favoritism. Also the higher award would have brought unwelcome media attention to the underwater demolition teams, which were deeply classified and unknown outside a small military circle.

Draper Jr. said, "My grandfather believed that if the award was sent to Congress for approval, the father-son connection would attract public attention for all the wrong reasons, harming the Navy and the war effort." Furthermore,

> I heard my grandfather cite two additional reasons, besides avoiding the appearance of favouritism. The first was Dad's private communication to him that giving the commanding officer of the team the Medal of Honor was inappropriate since the entire team shared the dangers and many of them had been as exposed as he was, or more so. My grandfather also said that a second Navy Cross would be just as meaningful if Dad stayed in the service (which of course he did). In addition, the Medal of Honor could eventually be a handicap for promotion to flag rank. It was so rarely given out that it was seen (at least in the Navy) as an award given only for extraordinary recklessness, which, as he said, "was not a characteristic much prized in potential admirals!" (Draper Kauffman Jr. correspondence, author's collection)

Draper Kauffman said that the subsequent award of the Legion of Merit (for actions in the invasion of Iwo Jima and Okinawa) had actually been of more help to him in terms of promotion than any of the awards for bravery.

After World War II Kauffman was involved with organizing the atomic bomb tests at Bikini Atoll and in radiological safety. He became naval aide to the secretary of the Navy and in 1960 was promoted to rear admiral. Kauffman became the forty-fourth superintendent of his alma mater, the U.S. Naval

Academy. His last assignment was as the commander of U.S. Naval Forces in the Philippines and representative of the commander in chief, Pacific, a post filled twenty-five years earlier by his father. He retired in 1973 with thirty-two years of service still never having passed the Navy's eye exam. He continued to smoke cigarettes and drink strong coffee, a habit from his tension-filled life in the war. Draper Kauffman died of a heart attack on a visit to Hungary in 1979, at the age of sixty-eight.

In March 1986 USS *Kauffman* (FFG 59) was christened in honor of father and son. The ship's coat of arms incorporates the Navy Cross each of them was awarded, as well as stars to denote their respective flag officer ranks. The central exterior ornament at the top of the crest is a bomb with lighted fuse to symbolize the younger Kauffman's remarkable career in UXB disposal as a volunteer in the Royal Navy, and his pioneering role as founder of the U.S. Navy's Explosive Ordnance Demolition program and Underwater Disposal Teams and the SEALS.

HM assignment: *King Alfred.*

Edmund Webster Kittredge. Born December 5, 1910, at the family home, "Ridgeway," one of the famous old Charlotte County, Virginia, plantations. Kittredge was discharged from the Royal Navy on June 24, 1946. Also in 1946 he married Virginia Champlin, an American who worked for the Office of Strategic Services (forerunner of the CIA), in London. The couple returned to the United States and took up residence in Rhode Island, the home state of his new wife, and started a family. He gave up banking. In 1960 Kittredge earned a master's degree in economics at Brown University and went on to teach economics in junior colleges until his retirement in 1972. Kittridge died in February 1980.

HM assignments: *Diomede, Copra, Cricket,* RN Commando "Easy" Company, Inchmarnock, *Armadillo, Dragonfly, Squid Hythe, Myloden.*

Carl Konow. Born 1899 in Copenhagen, Denmark. For the ten-day passage to England to join the Royal Navy, Konow embarked in a handsome motor yacht, HMS *Seaborn.* Following the liberation of Denmark on May 5, 1945, Konow was assigned as liaison officer on the staff of Rear Admiral Reginald Holt, RN, an old friend from yachting days in Bermuda in the 1930s. Konow finished the war in the rank of lieutenant commander. He went on to serve in the Royal Danish Naval Reserve from which he retired as a commander. His passion for yacht racing never abated and when he became too old to leap across decks he refereed and wrote about yachting. Konow married in 1945. He was a U.S. national who had also been offered British citizenship, but having married a Dane he decided to return to live in Denmark. After an adventuresome life he found it difficult to settle down to a domestic routine; the couple divorced a few years later. His two children say their parents remained good friends who cheerfully shared child-rearing duties and attended one another's parties. Neither parent remarried. Konow died on September 10, 1972, in Svendborg.

HM assignments: *Ausonia, LST 50, Prince Leopold,* and *LST 198* which he also commanded.

Derek Armitage Lee. Born in Englewood, New Jersey, on November 10, 1911, to Humphrey Armitage and Mary Davis. Lee actually gave his birthday as the 11th because 11/11/11 looked better. The family textile firm, Arthur H. Lee & Sons of Birkenhead, was founded in Bolton, Lancashire, in 1888 and, by the 1930s, operated in England and the United States. The English arm of the firm produced textiles of the highest quality using innovative production techniques and designs. Queen Elizabeth II wore robes of hand-loomed velvet made in Birkenhead by the Lee firm at her coronation in Westminster Abbey in 1952; subsequently, the company provided textiles for the White House and Blair House (the president's official guesthouse) during the Kennedy era. In 1965 the company merged with Johnson and Faulkner to form Lee Jofa.

Derek Lee is one of the officers who remained in the Royal Navy when the United States entered World War II, leaving in 1946 in the rank of lieutenant commander. During the war, his wife, Constance B., lived in Boston. After the war Lee entered the American side of the family business. For services as president of the British-American Chamber of Commerce, Lee was appointed Companion of the Most Excellent Order of the British Empire. He lived in New York City for the last twenty-five years of his life and retired in 1980. Lee died in Manhattan on April 11, 1985, at the age of seventy-three.

HM assignments: *Sardonyx, Braithwaite, Ferret, Saker, Bickerton, Ferret.*

John Matthew Leggat. Born December 7, 1918, in Los Angeles, California. Leggat was one of the few volunteers who came from west of the Mississippi. He was sent for training to HMS *Drake* instead of the Royal Naval College. Professionally well regarded and personally popular, the Royal Navy described him as an "efficient officer and good shipmate." Quite aware of his American nationality Leggat's superior wrote that "it reflects considerable credit on him that he joined the British Navy quite some time before the entry of the United States into the war." The Royal Navy's assessment concludes, "He has done much for Anglo-American co-operation, being well liked by all those with whom he has come into contact." Including his service in the U.S. Navy, by war's end his ribbons were typical of those who served in British and U.S. forces: the Royal Navy gave him the 1939–1945 Star and the Atlantic Star. From the United States he was awarded American Area Campaign Medal, Asiatic-Pacific Campaign Medal with two stars (stars denote specific campaigns), the Philippine Liberation Medal with one star, and the World War II Victory Medal.

In January 1946 Leggat transferred to the U.S. Naval Reserve with the rank of lieutenant commander and retained his commission for another dozen years while he worked on the civilian side of Naval Intelligence. Leggat married Margaret Daggett in June 1946. The GI Bill paid for his higher education and he graduated from Georgetown University's School of Foreign Service but did not enter the State Department. After 1962 he made a career in communications and marketing. Leggat died on May 26, 1992.

HM assignment: *Richmond, Woolston, LST 301, King Alfred, Richmond.*

Peter Greene Morison. Born April 6, 1917, in Concord, New Hampshire. The only son of Samuel Eliot Morison and Elizabeth Greene Shaw, Morison came from one of New England's most prominent families with ancestral roots deeply imbedded in Massachusetts history. Following family tradition, Peter Morison was schooled at St. Paul's (also attended by another of the Royal Navy's Americans, David Gibson). In England, Morrison met Judy Day and after a courtship they were married in fall 1942. Uncompromising in-laws and an uncertain young wife scuttled the relationship. Because of the mother-in-law's overpowering presence his wife refused to leave her mother and accompany her husband to the United States. Morison was released from

U.S. forces in late 1945. The couple divorced in 1948. In the years following Morison worked for the United Fruit Company in Central America, was appointed assistant to Angier Biddle Duke, chief of protocol in President John F. Kennedy's administration, and owned and operated a movie theater in Bar Harbor, Maine. He married three times and had three children. Peter Morison died of throat cancer on the island of St. Vincent in the Caribbean in March 1969.

Peter Morison's son Sam was born in London and retained dual U.S./British citizenship until February 1967. U.S. law requires all military commissioned officers to be U.S. citizens. Sam wrote, "Since I was one year away from being commissioned and I knew my grandfather [the imposing professor, award-winning historian, and rear admiral] would kill me if I didn't get commissioned, I renounced my British citizenship."

Of his parents' relationship, Sam recalls,

> I never saw my father until I was seventeen. The story is amusing. My grandmother and mother wanted to go shopping. They wanted me to come with them. I didn't want to. My grandmother, being a sly old fox said if I come we could stop at the King Cole Bar in the St. Regis Hotel in New York (East 55th) for tea and I could have all the hamburgers I liked. Well, I liked the hamburgers at the bar tremendously, so she hooked me. I was sitting with my back to the room, opposite my mother. My grandmother and mother were on a sofa in front of me with my mother directly opposite me. There was a huge mirror, rectangular in shape, above them that I could see into. Anyway, the two women were gabbing away and I was eating hamburgers. Everybody was happy. In between hamburger mouthfuls, I straightened up to catch my breath. I accidentally looked in the mirror and saw somebody that looked exactly like me. I figured it was an optical illusion and thought nothing of it. On my third hamburger I stopped again, accidentally looked in the mirror and saw the same thing. Now my grandmother was very strict that I could not interrupt any conversation unless she had stopped talking. She hadn't but this one I did with emphasis. I leaned over to my mother and I remember this as if it was yesterday, "there is a man sitting in the middle of the room that looks exactly like me. Who is he?" She looked over my left shoulder

> and said "My God! It's your father" and proceeded to get very flustered. That's the first conscious memory I have of seeing him. (Sam Morison correspondence, author's collection)

HM assignment: 782 Squadron, Royal Naval Air Station Hatston, Orkney.

John Stanley Parker. Born January 15, 1890, in Boston. Parker was the oldest son of Francis Stanley Parker and Harriet Amory Anderson. Following secondary schooling at one of New England's prestigious private schools, Groton, he entered Harvard University and graduated AB with honors in 1913. Shortly afterward he met Violet Otis Thayer, the elder daughter of the Reverend William Greenough Thayer, Head of St. Mark's School, and married her in autumn 1914 in the school chapel. The Reverend Thayer officiated at the wedding. Their first son was born in April 1916 and named Francis Stanley after John Parker's father who had died earlier that winter. Parker attended officers training camp at Plattsburg, near Lake Champlain in upstate New York. Camps like this produced 100,000 new officers, the "90-day wonders," for the U.S. Army in the First World War.

By 1917 the United States teetered on the brink of joining the Allies against the Central Powers when John Parker joined the staff of the Submarine Signal Company in Boston, working on listening devices. His leadership talents were evident, and by early 1918 he was an assistant general manager responsible for the Fessenden Engineering Laboratory, a division of the company. The job put him into close orbit with a legendary scientific personality in the field of wireless communications, Reginald Fessenden. An eccentric Canadian genius and Thomas Edison protégé, Fessenden was the first person to prove that voices and music could be sent over the air without wires. On Christmas Eve, 1906, radio operators on several United Fruit Company ships in the Atlantic heard Fessenden transmit a recording of Handel's "Largo" on an Ediphone, play "O, Holy Night" on his violin, and read from the Bible before wishing everyone a "Happy Christmas." Fessenden perfected his invention of the fathometer, developed a wireless system to permit submarines to signal one another, and invented a device that could bounce radio waves off icebergs (despite the war, no one had forgotten the catastrophic loss of the White Star Line's liner RMS *Titanic*). John Parker was among world-class pioneers. But something in his spirit left him discontented and restless.

In late March 1918, he quit his job and enlisted in the U.S. Navy as a seaman second class. Shortly after the birth of his second son he shipped out on USS *Colhoun* (DD 85), one of the Navy's new flush deck *Wickes*-class destroyers, a "four-piper," on active service escorting convoys to the Azores. Parker was an exemplary petty officer and by Christmas Eve he had been awarded a commission and the gold collar bars and single stripe of an ensign. (Twenty-three years later in the Royal Navy he met his fate on *Colhoun*'s sister ship.) In April 1919 he took his discharge and went back to work, this time for his uncle in the family firm, Hanson & Parker, in Boston. He worked there for several years, moved on to be a director with City Fuel Company, and then started a firm, Incorporated Investors, to distribute common stock. The financial crash of 1929 proved ruinous: after reimbursing his clients he shifted over to Hutchins and Parkinson as a "customers man."

Violet never remarried. A very old friend, a widower with six grown children, proposed to her but she refused him.

HM assignments: *Broadwater.*

The story is incomplete without an account of John Parker's two sons, Frank and John Jr. They were not RNVR volunteers but each of them was motivated by the same desire to fight a great menace and Frank, like Draper Kauffman, enrolled at the earliest opportunity in the army of France. And also like Kauffman, he was captured and made a POW. The youngest son, a U.S. Navy officer, was killed on a hostile beach in the Far East.

Francis Stanley Parker. The family called him Frank. John Parker's older son graduated from St. Mark's School in Southborough, Massachusetts, in 1935 and entered Harvard. He left in the spring of his freshman year to pursue life as an artist. All he had ever wanted to do was paint and study painting. The privilege and advantage of a Harvard education meant nothing to him. He rented a room on Beacon Hill in Boston and studied privately with Kleber Hall, who had taught him at St. Mark's. Frank next moved to Manhattan to study full-time at The Arts Students League. In New York he met the surrealist painter Giorgio de Chirico who wanted him to come to Rome. However, Frank was set on Paris and moved there in 1938 to live among other artists. The Giacometti brothers, Alberto and Diego, befriended him and Alberto became his mentor.

As the German army advanced on the city in 1940, Frank joined a volunteer French army ambulance unit, as Draper Kauffman had done. When French resistance collapsed Frank with twenty other members of the American Volunteer Corps crossed into Spain, which they thought might serve as an escape route. Colonel James Sparks, an Indianapolis physician, was the unit's commanding officer. They arrived in Spain wearing uniforms and decorations received from the French government. Spanish authorities promptly arrested and imprisoned them all until it could be determined whether they had served as combatant troops. Combatants would have been interned for the duration of the war. The group was taken to Barcelona, kept in a hotel there under arrest and later escorted to the Portuguese border and released.

The French army experience convinced Frank to join up almost at once when he returned. He enlisted in the Black Watch of Canada and was offered a commission. He declined the opportunity to become an officer because he wanted first to spend time in the ranks. A second chance never came. Frank was captured during the raid on Dieppe. His life was spared because chance placed him in the third wave to reach the Dieppe beaches. Soldiers in the first assaults were picked off immediately. Frank was in a small group of privates captured together. Even the German guards asked what the Allied commanders had been thinking when they planned the raid. Frank spent the remainder of the war in three different POW camps, including Stalag 8B in Pomerania where he did agricultural work in the shadow of a giant feudal estate. He was horsewhipped on one occasion and thrown into a latrine on another. A rifle stock put a lifelong scar on his forehead.

Another wound became infected while he was in prison camp. A menacing, black streak had started to climb up his inner arm. There were no doctors. He traded a couple packs of Red Cross parcel cigarettes for a bar of soap and a candle and used his wetted shirt, saturated with soap, to bind up the injured arm. Throughout the night he held a candle close to the shirt hoping that the primitive poultice would draw out the poison. It worked. By morning the ugly line was gone. Frank succeeded in his third escape attempt.

Within six weeks of being returned to England he met and married a Scot, Lesley Grey, with whom he had two daughters. They lived briefly in the south of France before resettling in Cambridge, Massachusetts, in the early 1950s. The marriage did not succeed. Frank next married an American, Judith

Wolfinsohn, in 1969. They had one daughter who said of her father, "He had a Victorian Boston accent. It was like being raised by somebody from a different century." Years later, when his daughter was grown, she asked him why he went to Canada to join up. Frank answered simply, "Hitler had to be stopped." Frank made his way as a painter, illustrator, and graphic artist. *The Boston Globe* described him as "a Boston blueblood with a working man's wardrobe and a poet's disregard for convention. He created lovely impressionistic paintings that were exhibited in the Boston Athenaeum" (obituary, *Boston Globe*, 3 March 2005). Frank was a lifelong friend of the poet Robert Lowell; his illustrations appear as frontispieces and jacket designs for Lowell's many books.

Frank Parker died on March 2, 2005, of complications from Parkinson's disease just a few weeks before his eighty-ninth birthday.

John Stanley Parker Jr. Born June 2, 1918, in Boston, Massachusetts. Gregarious like his father, John Jr. was the youngest son. He graduated from St. Mark's and Harvard University, class of '41, one of sixty graduates who were commissioned through the Reserve Officer Training Corps program. At Harvard he had been a member of the Hasty Pudding Club which voted him as having "the best legs in the chorus." When his father was killed on HMS *Broadwater* and Frank was reported missing in action after Dieppe it was John Jr. who held the fort and took care of his mother. He went on to Tufts University Medical School with the intention of becoming a psychiatrist but left two years later to join the U.S. Navy where he was commissioned an ensign in the unrestricted line, a sea officer like his father. He trained in naval mine warfare and mine disposal and was killed on May 14, 1945, during clearing operations connected with the invasion of Okinawa. Parker was on the beach collecting unexploded ordnance when he stumbled and fell, detonating whatever it was he had picked up. A colleague described the incident: "It was a small explosion, and the chief just a few feet behind was not badly hurt, but John's body took the full force" (correspondence dated 28 May 1945, Okinawa, Judith Parker collection). Long afterward, Frank said that his younger brother had ignored a cardinal superstition of the Navy, which is never to do someone else's job, even as a favor, unless ordered. John Jr. was supposed to have been aboard his ship. Small Bomb Disposal Unit #3 in Okinawa was named Camp Parker, in John's honor. When the inevitable War Department telegram came to her in Boston, Violet Parker had just received a message from her only remaining son, Frank, that he was in England en route home after being a prisoner of war. Besides her husband and a son, Violet lost a brother and a nephew in the war.

Charles Burnham Porter. Born July 27, 1906, at the family summer home in Beverly Farms, Massachusetts. On January 5, 1943, Porter transferred to American forces. His U.S. commission was helped by the intervention of an old yachting friend, Charles Francis Adams Jr. Adams was a lawyer and government official as well as the great-grandson of the sixth U.S. president. In September 1944 Porter was reassigned to stateside duties and promoted to lieutenant commander. In autumn 1946 he returned to Beverly Farms and the business of real estate as manager of R. M. Bradley & Co. He spent his leisure time sailing yachts and participated in the Bermuda and Halifax races and cruising in the Bahamas. He was a member of the Cruising Club of America and elected as its fleet captain (1947–48) and rear commodore of the Boston Station. Typical of his generation and wartime experiences he smoked and in 1993 underwent a lung resection due to cancer. He never married. Charles Burnham Porter died on September 6, 1995.

HM assignment: *Repulse*, Staff officer, commander in chief, The Nore.

Henry Fremont Ripley. Born November 28, 1904, at Camp Keithley, Mindanao, Philippines. Passed over for promotion Ripley left the U.S. Navy at the end of December 1945, in the rank of lieutenant commander. Ripley had eighteen years of service, two years less than the minimum needed for retirement on half pay. He settled near a sister in San Antonio, Texas, and worked briefly as a haberdashery salesman before becoming a schoolteacher. He never remarried. Henry Fremont Ripley died of cirrhosis on December 2, 1960.

HM assignments: *Nasturtium*.

Edwin Fairman Russell. Born 1914 in Elizabeth, New Jersey. Russell was educated at Newark Academy and Princeton University (class of 1937). In 1943 he transferred to the U.S. Navy and was a lieutenant commander on his release from active duty. In 1947 Russell took over his father's paper, Newark *Star-Ledger*. Later he became president and chairman of the Harrisonburg,

Pennsylvania, *Patriot-News,* which is a daily paper old enough to have covered Abraham Lincoln's visit to Union troops after the Battle of Gettysburg and publish Lincoln's famous eulogy. Patriotism and commitment to public service remained a driving force in Russell's life. He was Dwight Eisenhower's campaign manager in Pennsylvania in 1952 and traveled with Richard Nixon and Henry Kissinger to China. Divorced from Sarah Mary Churchill Russell, with whom he had four daughters, he married a first cousin of the mother of Diana, Princess of Wales, whose funeral he attended as a family member.

At the Greenwich ceremony in 2001 when the plaque naming all the volunteers was installed in the Painted Hall, Russell was the sole Royal Navy volunteer who was able to make the journey. Russell died at the age of eighty-seven on December 22, 2001, in Hobe Sound, Florida. In the following summer his wife, children, stepchildren, and grandchildren traveled to Normandy where they scattered his ashes on Omaha Beach.

HM assignments: *Maloja*, *Norfolk*.

John Albert Stilwell. Little is known about him, including dates of birth and death. Stilwell was the fourth—and only—American aviator in the volunteer group to train at the Royal Naval College. In spring 1943 he was with HMS *Asbury*, a Royal Navy shore station occupying the Berkley Carteret and Monterey hotels in New Jersey. In June he was with 845 Squadron. By August he was assigned to another shore base, HMS *Sparrowhawk*, in the Orkneys. When his unit deployed to Ceylon in early 1944 Stilwell remained in Northern Ireland. Somewhere in those years he suffered injuries to his leg when his aircraft crashed during carrier operations. He is among the Americans who did not transfer to U.S. forces.

HM assignments: *Asbury*, 845 Squadron, *Gadwall*.

William Erwin Gibson Taylor. Born July 4, 1905, in Fort Leavenworth, Kansas. In 1947 his name was forwarded to Under Secretary of State Dean Acheson for the post of Assistant Secretary of State for Air but the nomination did not succeed. In 1948 Taylor was awarded the Legion of Merit for his wartime work with Project Afirm involving the early deployment of radar in airborne intercepts. After retiring from the Naval Reserve on a medical disability because of infectious hepatitis contracted by a yellow fever shot, he worked as a terminal manager in Panama for Braniff Airlines until 1955 when he became vice president for political affairs for the Scandinavian Airline System. He retired a second time in 1970 and lived in Greece. In 1979 he moved back to the United States. There is an unverified rumor that he was engaged to American film actress Loretta Young. Young's tabloid-style and entirely vacuous autobiography does not mention him. Taylor never married.

Taylor kept detailed files on his military career including large, hardcover albums into which he carefully pasted the photographs, letters, and notes of his time in British forces. The collection is a valuable trove of a remarkable life in the pioneering age of aviation. With no wife or children to take an interest, at his death the papers would have been lost had it not been for his younger sister, Margaret. She directed Taylor's caregiver to gather them up and have them shipped to the Smithsonian's Air and Space Museum in Washington, D.C., where they are stored at the Garber Facility. Except for that, the whole personal record of his military life painstakingly maintained by Taylor might have been put at curbside, bundled with other unwanted paper for recycling. Taylor died a solitary and private man in St. Petersburg, Florida, on June 9, 1991.

HM assignments: *Curlew*, *Argus*, *Glorious*, *Furious*, *Ark Royal*, *Merlin*, *Sparrowhawk*, 804 Squadron.

David Arnold van Epps. Born October 20, 1915, in Chicago, Illinois. The only son of Frank and Pearl van Epps, David grew up in Williams Bay, Wisconsin, on the shores of Lake Geneva where he was a lifeguard during his high school years. Van Epps graduated with a BA degree from the University of Wisconsin in 1938. He resigned his commission in the RNVR on July 1, 1943, and transferred to the U.S. Army Air Corps. Van Epps returned to the United States in October 1945 and made a career of the U.S. Air Force from which he retired in 1963 as a lieutenant colonel. After a whirlwind romance lasting a matter of weeks he married Helen Nielsen. They had a daughter, Chris. The marriage failed. He then married Ann who brought him a stepdaughter, Michelle. David Van Epps died of ALS, amyotrophic lateral sclerosis (Lou Gehrig's disease), on October 12, 1975, in Elkhorn, Wisconsin.

HM assignments: *Victorious*, *Raven*, *Heron*, *Blackcap*, *Landrail*, 760 Squadron, 894 Squadron, 759 Squadron, 809 Squadron.

John Gilbert Winant served as ambassador to the Court of St. James until 1946. He helped to plan the Teheran conference that set the pattern for the postwar world, as well as the plan for the Allied occupation of Germany. At his instigation, the first committee to investigate Axis war crimes was established in summer 1942. Besides entertaining U.S. troops he developed close relations with all walks of British life, from the ordinary "bloke" in the street to the Royal Family. Winston Churchill said of him, "Mr. Winant always put the American point of view with force and clarity and argued his country's case with vigor, but his constant purpose was to smooth away the difficulties and prevent misunderstanding and he always gave us the feeling of how gladly he would give his life to see the good cause triumph. He was a friend of justice truth and freedom" (John G. Winant biographical sketch by Rivington G. Winant, Franklin & Eleanor Roosevelt Institute).

After the war President Harry Truman appointed Winant to be U.S. representative to UNESCO. Winant had an easy smile and was a lifelong teetotaler but not a scold. He was also a man haunted by difficulties he never overcame, like bouts of depression and fear of public speaking—which terrified him though he was well received because what he had to say mattered to people. Winant died on November 3, 1947, and is buried on the grounds of his old school, St. Paul's.

APPENDIX III

Napoleon to Kaiser: Americans in British and Other Service

The World War II RNVR volunteers were not the first of their countrymen to freely join with England in a fight. In 1805 twenty-three Americans served with Admiral Horatio Nelson at the Battle of Trafalgar. The first American to be awarded a Victoria Cross was twenty-four-year-old William Henry Harrison Seeley from Topsham, Maine. In 1860 a family disagreement propelled him all the way to the Pacific, possibly as crew aboard a British merchantman and he transferred to the Royal Navy on the China Station. On September 6, 1864, in front of the batteries at Shimonoseki, Japan, Ordinary Seaman Seeley of HMS *Euryalus* distinguished himself by a daring reconnaissance of enemy positions and, although wounded, he continued to take part in the final assault on the battery. Following his discharge, he returned home.

For sheer numbers of volunteers willing to put on another country's uniform, the last century stands alone. In 1914 "The call to the colors of the various warring nations quickly drew into the conflict those who . . . have expressed the allegiance of sympathy if not of birth," wrote the editor of a book quickly compiled to list the first Harvard University volunteers in World War I. By the time the book was printed in 1916, twenty Harvard men (not including a German graduate who was killed in action) had fallen in a war in which their government had maintained steadfast neutrality (M. A. DeWolfe Howe, ed., *The Harvard Volunteers in World War I*, Boston: Harvard University Press, 1916).

Upwards of 35,000 men of American origin served with the Canadian Expeditionary Force, and five of them were awarded the Victoria Cross: Frederick Coppins, San Francisco, California; Bellenden Hutchison, Mt. Carmel, Illinois; William Metcalf, Lewiston, Maine; George Mullin, Portland, Oregon; and Raphael Zengel, Fairbault, Minnesota. Exact numbers of volunteers are elusive because the men disguised their U.S. citizenship by giving ethnic origins as their nationality and the YMCA as their address. Some were resident in Canada when war was declared in August 1914. Others crossed the border to enlist. There were whole American battalions and even a designated American Legion in the Canadian forces sent to fight in France. Chicago-born Raymond Chandler, creator of the famous fictional detective Philip Marlow, served in the 50th Regiment of Victoria and was wounded. William Faulkner was a lieutenant in the Canadian Royal Flying Corps. Harvard's little book of first-person narratives sketched the background of 400-plus alumni who participated in various branches of foreign service. The men were scattered throughout Allied forces, often as drivers with the American Hospital Ambulance Corps, but also in Belgian, French, and British military uniform.

Among the first to enlist in 1914 against the Kaiser were New Yorkers William E. Dugan from Rochester, New York, who joined the French Foreign Legion, and Arnold Whitridge from New Rochelle, New York, an enlistee in the Anglo-American Corps. Whitridge's grandfather was the celebrated English poet Matthew Arnold. There was also Major Julian Day from Rye, New York, who received a Military Cross while serving with the West Kents at Gallipoli. Virginia surgeon Vivian Slaughter of Orange township, New Jersey, "died gloriously going straight for a German machine gun" (L. S. M. Robinson, ed., "Lest We Forget," *Sea Power Magazine*, Navy League of the United States).

The oldest to enlist was another New Yorker, Charles F. Mitchell, sixty-one years of age. He became a corporal in the Army Service Corps, in London. The youngest was fifteen-year-old Clarence M. McGrew (Canadian 1st Division) from South Bend, Indiana, who was killed in action at age sixteen while carrying dispatches during the Battle of Cambrai. G. W. Covington Jr. came from Montgomery, Alabama, to serve with the Gloucesters, and S. M. Armstrong from Woburn, Massachusetts, got his first wound on July 4, 1916, during the "Big Push." In all he was wounded four times and also suffered dysentery and trench fever. Armstrong repeatedly declined a commission "as it would have necessitated giving up American citizenship" (ibid., issues July–December 1919).

The Duchess de Talleyrand recruited Dr. David Wheeler who left his practice in Manhattan for the Foreign Legion and was badly wounded in the leg. While crawling back to his unit on hands and knees, he stopped to dress the wounds and give morphine to men lying under fire. Ambulances passed but he refused to be taken up while there was still work to do. His own wound was gangrenous by the time he reached a hospital. He survived, as did George Gillespie from Philadelphia, Pennsylvania, serving with the 15th Argyll and Sutherland Highlanders, who was poisoned by chlorine gas at Mametz Wood.

Captain Owen Lobb Holleran of Atlanta, Georgia, who joined the Royal Dublin Fusiliers, was wounded and had both feet frozen on the Serbian expedition. One foot was amputated. He soldiered on and as a pilot in the Royal Flying Corps he was wounded again and captured. Ernest Hemingway, denied entry into U.S. military service due to vision problems, joined the French army as an ambulance driver. This was the path followed by Draper Kauffman in World War II, and for the same physical handicap: less than 20/20 vision. Reassigned by the French to support Italian troops, Hemingway was wounded by Austrian artillery fire. His novel *A Farewell to Arms* came out of the experience.

A rare but much more organized initiative, well funded and with a clearly defined purpose, was the recruitment launched by Consuelo Vanderbilt Balsan. *The Glitter and the Gold* describes an especially famous group of American volunteers. She explained, "During the war Jacques [Colonel Jacques Balsan, her second husband] commanded a group of scout planes. In 1915 he, together with my father, William K. Vanderbilt [who undertook to pay for the transport of any American who wished to fight in the French air force], and Dr. Goss of the American Hospital at Neuilly, raised a squadron piloted by American aviators." On April 20, 1916, the French government designated the group N-214 and called it the Escadrille Americaine. It was quickly sent to the Western sector for active service on the front lines. Following German protests over the name (the United States was neutral until April 6, 1917), the squadron was renamed Escadrille Lafayette.

The escadrille started with seven American pilots. Its inaugural combat mission was May 13, 1916. The first aerial kill occurred five days later when Kiffen Rockwell shot down a German two-seater LVG biplane. Victor Chapman, a Harvard graduate, and Norman Prince were the escadrille's first fatalities, killed in action a little over a month later. The unit recorded fifty-seven kills and gained legendary fame that has endured to modern times. American volunteers flocked to join. Following the United States' formal entry in the war the escadrille passed to the U.S. Army. By then, nine men had lost their lives. Admiration for the escadrille fired the imagination of American schoolboys, including the RNVR volunteers in World War II.

Thrown out of the U.S. Naval Academy in his senior year because of heavy drinking, Merian C. Cooper was a fighter pilot in World War I. Convinced that no one could survive the ball of plummeting fire that had been Cooper's aircraft disappearing behind enemy lines, the U.S. Army issued Cooper's family a death certificate. But it was not his time. He went on to other aerial exploits and also to make a significant mark in Hollywood films. In the 1920s Cooper, a passionate anticommunist, joined the volunteer Kosciusko Squadron of Americans flying combat missions in Poland's fight against Bolshevist Russia. Poland bestowed its highest award for gallantry on Cooper. Today he is remembered for producing several fine motion pictures including, *The Quiet Man*, *Rio Grande*, *The Searchers*, and, most famously, *King Kong*, which he also wrote and directed. Cherry, van Epps, Taylor, Konow, and Homans probably shaped their pilot aspirations on the feats of daring-do in Cooper's 1927 film *Wings* (the first film to win an Academy Award for "Best Picture") and *Hell's Angels* three years later, in which Cooper was also one of the wartime aces employed to fly the stunts.

APPENDIX IV

How the Story Came to Be Told

Ronald E. "Chalky" White had retired from the Sussex Police after thirty years' service and was working in West Sussex, at the Magistrates Court in Worthing. Having been a Boy Seaman in the early 1950s, Chalky grew from adolescence to maturity in the Royal Navy. The experience ignited a lifetime passion for ships and the sea, spiced with an abiding love of naval history. In his spare time he started to organize a service of remembrance for HMS *Broadwater* at the Church of St. Mary's in the area of Worthing known as Broadwater, after which the ship had been named. It was while researching the World War II warship that he happened to pick up *Yankee RN* by Commander Alex H. Cherry, OBE, RNVR, that had been on his shelf for many years and noticed the dedication to John Stanley Parker. The book mentions the commemorative plaque in the Painted Hall. This was in about 1998 and marks the start of the most productive phase of the effort to identify the U.S. citizens who served in the Royal Naval Volunteer Reserve in World War II.

Chalky was intrigued to find more information about Parker and Cherry and the others who came to England at that perilous time. Then he had a significant stroke of luck. Charlotte Hammond, a practicing solicitor, was a clerk at the Magistrates Court and a friend. Her father owned a printing company and Chalky asked if he could publish a program for the church service. Some twenty years earlier Police Constable White had led the funeral procession for the Duke of Norfolk through the streets of Arundel, and Chalky remembered that Charlotte's father had been responsible for the design and printing of the elegant order of service. After Chalky explained his project to Charlotte the two became instant, firm friends and research partners. The St. Mary's service was a success. By this time, Chalky and Charlotte had started to wonder how many more American volunteers there might have been.

In the United Kingdom, a man's service record is virtually inaccessible, unlike the United States where information is released according to a time scale to protect privacy, but not hide confirmation of ordinary military details. Chalky and Charlotte wrote hundreds of letters to museums, institutes, universities, and other establishments. They made multiple visits to Britain's National Archives and relied on the goodwill and interest of many people. It was a slog. Charlotte's aunt in Philadelphia helped with the detective work. John Parker's son Frank was traced through his prep school, Groton, and Harvard University. The surnames of some of the Greenwich men mentioned in *Yankee RN* led to a search of files in Britain's National Archives (formerly the Public Records Office).

Frank's wife, Judy, searched through the trove of Parker family papers and could confirm some of the identities if names were provided. For example, when asked about Homans. "Oh, yes!" came the response, "Homans is well known in Boston and he's a family friend." Judy also knew Emily Morison Beck, Peter Morison's sister. The Boston volunteers came from a tight-knit community and on occasion a name was sufficient for the Parkers to add more information or a lead to a relative.

But a good number of names came from outside Boston. Notices were posted in Navy magazines and Web sites. David Gibson was found through his ex–Royal Navy shipmate, an Englishman with whom he had maintained friendly contact. Ed Russell's name came from Winston Churchill Jr. who said at once that Russell was a cousin by marriage. Every Ferris in New York City was sent a letter, to no avail. The family history Web site uncovered one of the cousins. Another Ferris cousin was a director of Mattel, who was more fascinated by the fact we had found a connection and had managed to trace him. Draper Kauffman's story came via the people search engine. The son put us in touch with his father's sister, Beth Bush.

The U.S. Social Security death index was searched. The index lists the state of residence and there was always a chance that a family member still lived in the state. Everyone with the same surname in that state was written a letter. The National Personnel Records Center in St. Louis, Missouri, and a helpful assistant searched the database for the name of every volunteer we knew about and records were obtained of those who had transferred to U.S. forces. In turn, center documents hinted at other places to look. There were serendipitous discoveries.

At Greenwich, the director of planning mentioned a visit to the Painted Hall by a bank executive at J. P. Morgan, Mike Sabatell. A search of the Internet provided his contact details at the bank and a voicemail was left. He called back and told us more about Cherry, who was his godfather. Mike provided a copy of a 1977 U.S. Naval Institute *Proceedings* article by Lieutenant Eric Berryman, USN, and every Eric Berryman in the United States got a letter. As a result, the author of that article joined the team. A Derek Lee was found by chance after the Greenwich service when the name showed up on a real estate Web site in the Bahamas. He was e-mailed and luck held: he was the son. Judy Parker said that Charles Porter had a nephew. She did not know his name but recalled that both uncle and nephew were keen sailors. A letter was sent to a sailing club Porter had once belonged to, and that lead to his nephew. Every Kittredge in Rhode Island got a letter.

The initial effort to identify the men alluded to on the Painted Hall's mysterious plaque began in 1975 and had nothing to do with a ceremony. The late Commander Roland "Bud" Bowler, the USNI's chief executive and publisher, hoped to find the names and enough biographical detail for a vignette in the Old Navy section of *Proceedings.* He contacted Berryman, then a junior officer stationed at the Pentagon, showed him a photograph of the plaque and asked if the names of the three anonymous U.S. citizens could be found. Eric's assignment brought him access to the Office of the Secretary of the Navy, the U.S. Navy's highest civilian official, and Commander Bowler hoped the office could apply some leverage to persuade the Royal Navy to share personnel information, perhaps even a list. Sometimes the unofficial-official Old Boy circuit can produce significant results unavailable by other means. The secretary of the Navy of the day was Bill Middendorf, who was and remains a keen student of naval history. He gave his enthusiastic support at once. The Royal Navy was not so easily moved. There were veiled allusions to a couple of black sheep. Issues of privacy remained and only fourteen names were divulged, with scant personal details. The leads led to Draper Kauffman, Ed Russell, and Bill

Homans, all of whom cheerfully agreed to be interviewed and donate photographs of themselves in RNVR uniform.

With the discovery of twenty-one names (the twenty-second name, Surgeon Lieutenant Francis Hayes, was the last to be found), by early 2001 Chalky decided, with Charlotte's help, to organize a commemoration of the American volunteers at the Old Royal Naval College. The director of the Greenwich Foundation, the college's new owner, greeted his visitors with a genial, "Oh, so you're the Chalky White who has been writing to everyone." His characterization was not inaccurate. Also present was the director of planning. It was agreed that they would accommodate a ceremony in the college chapel.

Each year several hundred thousand visitors pass through the buildings and grounds where England trained her sea officers in naval science, beginning in 1873. In 1998 the Royal Navy moved to a new facility at Shrivenham, and responsibility for maintenance passed to the Greenwich Foundation. Today the venerable collection of buildings first planned by the architect Sir Christopher Wren is known as the Old Royal Naval College. There is much to admire, especially in the Painted Hall, a Baroque masterpiece. Here for three days from January 4, 1806, the body of Admiral Lord Nelson lay in state. More than 100,000 people walked past his bier to pay their last respects. In the annals of British naval history the magnificent, aptly named hall is a holy place. In the United States the equivalent, but on a much smaller scale, is the crypt at the Naval Academy in Annapolis where John Paul Jones' remains lie in a marble sarcophagus.

Setting aside space in the Painted Hall to honor the American volunteers was a gesture of special respect and affection by the Royal Navy and the British people.

Winston Churchill Jr. came aboard at around this time and quickly became one of the project's prime movers. His American great-grandmother was the mother of the wartime prime minister, Winston's grandfather and namesake. Winston chaired a planning committee. He also brought along his cousin Serena Balfour, Ed Russell's daughter. Serena's commitment proved to be pivotal. The fifth member of the committee was the Honorable Tim Lewin, son of the late Admiral of the Fleet Lord Lewin of Greenwich. Lord Lewin, who said that the mystery of the plaque provided "great after-dinner conversation," had helped Chalky with the St. Mary's commemoration. Tim applied the same creative enthusiasm after his father died and, together with Winston, opened doors that would otherwise have remained locked. Admiral Sir Benjamin Bathurst, head of the Greenwich Foundation, was supportive and slowly the project to install a new plaque began to take shape.

Research has continued down to the eve of publication. The store of information on the American volunteers steadily increased. There were further conversations with Ed Russell and David Gibson. Kauffman's sister obtained for us an endorsement from the former U.S. president and naval aviator, George H. W. Bush. Serena Balfour was a formidable ally before whom all real or threatening impediments receded like snow in springtime.

On October 3, 2001, the ceremony for the installation and dedication of the new plaque brought admirals, commodores, captains, and ratings from the United States Navy and the Royal Navy. The Archbishop of Canterbury, head of the Church of England, attended. Less than a month before, the world had been reminded anew that together we still face those who detest democracy and who would destroy us. The dignitaries stood together in ranks with veterans of the war at sea, 1939–45. The Royal Marine Band played on the Grand Square.

The new stone is bigger than its World War II companion because the names are all there. Not just the Ferris-Porter-Parker trio who made such a deep impression on the college's wartime faculty, but all twenty-two volunteers. There may be others and it would be an impertinence to make a definitive claim to the contrary. But after more than thirty years of searching we are "cautiously optimistic" that the list is complete.

Twenty-two silver presentation ingots were given to the guests most immediately connected to the volunteers. Only Ed Russell could be there in person. David Gibson, the one other surviving RNVR volunteer, was too ill to travel. The ingots were engraved, "In memory of those Americans who, between 1939–1941—when the fate of Great Britain, and of the cause of Freedom, hung in the balance—volunteered to serve in the Royal Navy."

On October 2, 2002, a service of thanksgiving was held at Chichester Cathedral in remembrance of HMS *Broadwater*, on which John Parker was killed. Prime Minister Tony Blair wrote, "This day commemorates the sinking of a gallant ship with heavy loss of life . . . [and] serves as a symbol of our lasting friendship between our two nations and a reminder of our united purpose then and now in the defense of freedom." Prayers were offered for all who still bear the marks of conflict in mind or body, and for all who are bereaved.

The commemoration continues in other ways, also. At Broadwater Manor School the silver HMS *Broadwater* Memorial Cup, sponsored by Caffyn's, is presented to the pupil who enters the best history project. The first winners were two eleven-year-olds, Clare Avery and Christopher Jeffs.

On June 22, 2004, the Old Royal Naval College hosted another related event: a service of remembrance for the men who lost their lives on HMS *Veteran*, including Surgeon Lieutenant Francis Mason Hayes, MRCS, LRCP, RNVR. The organist played Elgar's *Nimrod* from Enigma Variations. Prince Michael of Kent was the principal speaker. He said, "No man can do more for another country than volunteer to fight for it." A Royal British Legion bugler sounded Last Post. John Hayes placed a wreath in memory of the father he never knew.

The prime force behind the commemorations, Chalky White, died in the early morning hours of Saturday, May 23, 2009. He had mesothelioma, a rare form of lung cancer that comes from exposure to asbestos. Asbestos lagging had been much in use, especially in the engine spaces, in the World War II–era warships he served aboard. There is some irony in the likely cause of his death because May 23 marks the anniversary of the Royal Navy's first steam-powered vessel, *Comet,* introduced in 1822. The First Lord was provoked to issue a dire warning: "Their Lordships," he announced, "feel it their bounden duty to discourage to the utmost of their ability the employment of steam vessels, as they consider that the introduction of steam is calculated to strike a fatal blow at the naval supremacy of the empire."

Chalky was devoted to foot propulsion and covered his beloved Sussex countryside with long-distance hikes.

A falling star marks on the hill,
The path some long dead shepherd trod;
The song fades low, the shadows go,
And I,—I make my peace with God.

Burton Baldry, 1922

BIBLIOGRAPHY

BOOKS

Balsan, Consuelo Vanderbilt. *The Glitter and the Gold.* New York: Harper, 1952.

Barger, Melvin. *"Large Slow Target": A History of the Landing Ship Tanks (LST) and the Men Who Sailed Them.* Toledo: U.S. LST Association, 1986.

Barnett, Correlli. *Engage the Enemy More Closely: The Royal Navy in the Second World War.* London: Hodder and Stoughton, 1991.

Beauchamp, Cari. *Joseph P. Kennedy Presents: His Hollywood Years.* New York: Knopf, 2009.

Bellush, Bernard. *He Walked Alone: A Biography of John Gilbert Winant.* The Hague: Mouton, 1968.

Billingham, Elizabeth. *America's First Two Years: The Story of American Volunteers in Britain, 1939–1941.* London: John Murray, 1942.

Bush, Elizabeth K. *America's First Frogman—The Draper Kauffman Story.* Annapolis: U.S. Naval Institute, 2001.

Caine, Philip D. *American Pilots in the RAF: The WWII Eagle Squadrons.* London: Brassey's, 1998.

Canetti, Elias. *Party in the Blitz: The English Years.* New York: New Directions, 2005.

Cherry, Alex H. *Yankee RN: Being the Story of a Wall Street Banker Who Volunteered for Active Duty in the Royal Navy before America Came into the War.* London: Jarrolds, 1951.

Churchill, Winston S. *The Second World War.* 6 vols. London: Cassell, 1948–54.

Collingwood, Donald. *The Captain Class Frigates in the Second World War: An Operational History of the American-Built Destroyer Escorts Serving under the White Ensign, 1943–46.* London: Leo Cooper, 1998.

Costello, John, and Terry Hughes. *The Battle of the Atlantic.* London: Collins, 1977.

Franklin, Bruce Hamilton. *The Buckley-Class Destroyer Escorts.* London: Chatham Publishing, 1999.

Gaffen, Fred. *Cross-Border Warriors: Canadians in American Forces/Americans in Canadian Forces, from the Civil War to the Gulf War.* Toronto: Dundrum Press, 1995.

Goodhart, Philip. *Fifty Ships that Saved the World: The Foundation of the Anglo-American Alliance.* Garden City: Doubleday, 1965.

Harrison, Michael. *Rosa.* London: Peter Davies, 1962.

Haugland, Vern. *The Eagle Squadrons: Yanks in the RAF, 1940–1942.* New York: Ziff-Davis Flying Books, 1979.

Horne, Alistair. *La Belle France: A Short History.* New York: Knopf, 2005.

Howarth, Stephen. *The Royal Navy's Reserves in War and Peace, 1903–2003.* Barnsley: Leo Cooper, 2003.

Howe, M. A. DeWolfe, ed. *The Harvard Volunteers in Europe: Personal Records of Experience in Military, Ambulance, and Hospital Service.* Cambridge: Harvard University Press, 1916.

Kerr, J. Lennox, and Wilfred Granville. *The R.N.V.R.: A Record of Achievement.* London: George G. Harrap, 1957.

Kerr, J. Lennox, and David James, eds. *Wavy Navy* [A collection of writings by members of the R.N.V.R.]. London: George G. Harrap, 1950.

Kurson, Robert. *Shadow Divers: The True Adventure of Two Americans Who Risked Everything to Solve One of the Last Mysteries of World War II.* New York: Random House, 2004.

Lenton, H. T. *British and Empire Warships of the Second World War.* Annapolis: U.S. Naval Institute Press, 1998.

Lund, Paul, and Harry Ludlam. *The War of the Landing Craft.* London: Foulsham, 1976.

Macdermott, Brian. *Ships without Names: The Story of the Royal Navy's Tank Landing Ships of World War Two.* London: Arms and Armour, 1993.

Masters, Anthony. *Rosa Lewis: An Exceptional Edwardian.* New York: St. Martin's Press, 1978.

McCart, Neil. *HMS* Victorious *1937–1969.* Cheltenham: Fan Publications, 1998.

McElheran, Brock. *V-Bombs and Weathermaps: Reminiscences of World War II.* Montreal: McGill-Queen's University Press, 1995.

Messenger, Charles. *The Last Prussian: A Biography of Field Marshal Gerd von Rundstedt, 1875–1953.* London: Brassey's, 1991.

Middleton, Judy. *HMS* King Alfred, *1939–1945.* Hove: Judy Middleton, 1986.

Morison, Samuel Eliot. *The Atlantic Battle Won: May 1943–May 1945.* Boston: Little Brown, 1956.

———. *The Two-Ocean War.* Boston: Little Brown, 1963.

Pack, S. W. C. *Operation HUSKY: The Allied Invasion of Sicily.* New York: Hippocrene Books, 1977.

Paine, Lincoln P. *Ships of the World: An Historical Encyclopedia.* Boston: Houghton Mifflin, 1997.

Reed, James H. *Convoy "Maniac"—R.B. 1.* Lewes, Sussex: Book Guild, 2000.

Reed, Ken C. *The Hand-Me-Down Ships: This Is the True Account of the World War II Exploits of Ten Ex-American Coast Guard Cutters and the Officers and Men of the Royal Navy Who Served in Them.* Spalding: Reed, 1993.

Roskill, S. W. *The War at Sea 1939–1945.* Vol. 1, *The Defensive.* Uckfield: Naval and Military Press, 2004.

Scott, Peter. *The Battle of the Narrow Seas: The History of the Light Coastal Forces in the Channel and North Sea, 1939–1945.* London: Country Life, 1945.

Showell, Jak P. Mallmann. *Countermeasures against U-boats, Monthly Reviews: Annotated Extracts from Secret British Wartime Anti-submarine Reports.* Milton Keynes, Buckinghamshire: Military Press, 2002.

———. *The U-boat Offensive, Monthly Reviews: Annotated Extracts from Secret British Wartime Anti-submarine Reports.* Milton Keynes, Buckinghamshire: Military Press, 2003.

———. *What Britain Knew and Wanted to Know about U-boats, Including an Essential Summary of the Famous U-boat Commander's Handbook: Annotated Extracts from Secret British Wartime Anti-submarine Reports.* Milton Keynes, Buckinghamshire: Military Press, 2001.

Shrubb, R. E. A., and A. B. Sainsbury. *The Royal Navy Day by Day.* Fontwell: Centaur Press, 1979.

Stanford, Alfred. *Force Mulberry: The Planning and Installation of the Artificial Harbor off U.S. Normandy Beaches in World War II.* New York: William Morrow, 1951.

Sturtivant, Ray, and Theo Ballance. *The Squadrons of the Fleet Air Arm.* Tunbridge Wells: Air-Britain, 1994.

Sturtivant, Ray, and Mick Burrow. *Fleet Air Arm Aircraft 1939 to 1945.* Tunbridge Wells: Air-Britain, 1995.

Sweeney, Charles. *Sweeney: The Autobiography of Charles Sweeney.* Canterbury: Harrop Press, 1990.

Terraine, John. *Business in Great Waters: The U-Boat Wars 1916–1945.* London: Wordsworth Editions, 1999.

Turner, John Frayn. *Service Most Silent: The Navy's Fight against Enemy Mines.* London: George G. Harrap, 1955.

U.S. Navy. *Dictionary of American Naval Fighting Ships.* 8 vols. Washington, D.C.: Naval History Division, Department of the Navy, 1960–1981.

Vaz, Mark Cotta. *Living Dangerously: The Adventures of Merian C. Cooper, Creator of King Kong.* New York: Villard, 2005.

Wildenberg, Thomas. "An Eagle with Wings of Gold: The Remarkable Career of Bill Taylor." *Air Power History,* September 22, 2001. Air Force Historical Foundation: Andrews Air Force Base, Maryland.

Winant, John Gilbert. *Letter from Grosvenor Square: An Account of a Stewardship.* London: Hodder and Stoughton, 1947.

Winton, John. *Carrier Glorious: The Life and Death of an Aircraft Carrier*. London: Cooper, 1986.

Young, Loretta. *The Things I Had to Learn*. New York: Bobbs-Merrill, 1961.

ARTICLES

"100 Who Shaped the Century." [John Gilbert Winant]. *Concord Monitor*, Dec. 16, 1999.

Bellefontaine, Edgar J. "Enigmatic Giant: An Appreciation of William P. Homans, Jr." *Massachusetts Lawyers Weekly*, June 16, 1997.

Bloom, Harold. "Don Quixote at 400." *Wall Street Journal*, February 23, 2005.

Bradley, Mary O. "*Patriot-News* Delivers for 150 Years: Presses Roll through Mergers, Moves, Change." *Patriot-News* (Harrisburg, Pa.), March 7, 2004.

Bush, Eric, et al. "Naval Operations in Ramree Island Area 19th January to 22nd February, 1945." *Supplement to the London Gazette*, April 23, 1948. Despatch number 38269.

Engle, Paul M. "Danger Zone." Letter to the Editor. *Military Officer* magazine, September 2006, p. 14.

"John Gilbert Winant." *Current Biography*. New York: H. W. Wilson, 1941.

"The Law: Counsel for the G.I. Defense." *Time*, October 19, 1970.

"National Affairs: North of the Border." *Time*, July 15, 1940.

"National Defense: AIR: Aid to Britain." *Time*, December 2, 1940.

"Naturalized in the Field." *Time*, May 17, 1943.

Thomas, Robert McG., Jr. "William Homans Jr. Dies; Civil Rights Lawyer Was 75," *New York Times*, February 13, 1997.

"World Battlefronts: Battle of the Pacific: Ahoha." *Time*, July 6, 1942.

"World War: Eagles for Britain." *Time*, October 21, 1940.

"World War: Eagles Swoop." *Time*, July 14, 1941.

INTERNET RESOURCES

Boudreau, Dan. "Why Americans Served in the Canadian Expeditionary Force of World War One: The Aspect of Masculinity." wwu.edu/history/annual/papers/Boudreau.htm.

Felknor, Bruce L. "D-Day Plus 60 Years." *American Merchant Marine at War*. www.usmm.org/felknordday.html.

Hasslinger, Karl M. "The U-boat War in the Caribbean: Opportunities Lost." Newport: Naval War College, 1995. http://ibiblio.org/hyperwar/ETO/Atlantic/UBoat-Caribbean.html.

Kipling, S. H. "The Royal Naval Commandos." Royal Naval Commando Association. www.combinedops.com/RN%20Commando.htm.

"Lord Haw Haw and the Blackshirts." Contributed by Angela and Dianna. July 29, 2003. www.bbc.co.uk/ww2peopleswar/stories/78/a1126478.shtml.

"Memoirs of a Typical Teenager [Jim Bacon]." Contributed by SVC_Cambridge. May 27, 2005. www.bbc.co.uk/ww2peopleswar/stories/86/a4123586.shtml.

"Memories: A Child in Lewisham." Contributed by Thurza Blurton. March 18, 2004.

Schneller, Robert J. "The Genesis of the Minority Recruiting Program at the U.S. Naval Academy, 1965–1976." *International Journal of Naval History* 1:1 (2002). www.ijnhonline.org/volume1_number1_Apr02/pdf_april02/Final%20set/pdf_schneller1.pdf.

"A Telegram, a Trenchcoat and the Sinking of HMS *Broadwater*." Contributed by David Scott. August 5, 2005. BBC, *WW2 People's War*. www.bbc.co.uk/ww2peopleswar.

Universal News. "Premier Inspects London American Guard." [Newsreel of General Wade H. Hayes]. www.youtube.com/watch?v=HDBCtD6n3yE.

U.S. Navy Department. "Proceedings of the Hart Inquiry, Wednesday, April 26, 1944, Thirtieth Day." www.ibiblio.org/pha/pha/hart/hart-30.html.

INDEX

ABOUT THE AUTHORS

Eric Dietrich-Berryman was born in Berlin and grew up in Aberdare, Glamorgan, Wales, and Gloucester, England. He came to the United States at the age of seventeen as an unaccompanied immigrant on the German quota for 1957. He was educated at Upfield Preparatory School, Stroud; Hofstra University, New York (BA, 1966); and the University of New Mexico (MA, 1968; PhD, 1971). He served in the U.S. Army as a helicopter door gunner in the Mekong Delta region during the Vietnam War and retired from the U.S. Navy in 1994 as a commander. He retired a second time in 2003 from what is now the National Geospatial Intelligence Agency. Eric and his wife Bobbie live at the western foot of Cape Henry in Virginia.

Charlotte Hammond was born in Brighton, England. She spent her early years in Hove in a flat that overlooked HMS *King Alfred*. Educated at Chatsmore Catholic High School and Worthing Sixth Form College, she was Head Girl of her secondary school. She completed her professional studies at the College of Law, Guildford, and is now an associate solicitor, Commercial Litigation Department, in the Sea Lane Chambers of Bennett Griffin, Solicitors. Her paternal grandfather served in the plans section of the U.S. Navy's Grosvenor Square facility cited in this book, and afloat on the destroyer USS *Barton* and the cruiser USS *Columbus*. She was formerly a legal advisor in Court Service, where she met Police Constable Ronald White. She lives in Worthing with her daughter Sophie, son Joe, and partner Matthew Wrighton.

Ronald E. White, known to everyone as Chalky, was born in 1937 and educated at Cobham in Surrey. He entered the Royal Navy at the age of fifteen as a boy seaman and continued his education and naval training at HMS *St Vincent*, Gosport. Chalky served on board ships all over the world, including the destroyer HMS *Barrosa*, the frigate HMS *Troubridge,* and the aircraft carrier HMS *Victorious*. He joined Sussex Police in 1962 and served in various postings including Steyning, Shoreham-by-Sea, Arundel, Eridge, where he was the village police officer, and finally at Littlehampton, all within the County of Sussex. Chalky admired and respected the late Bernard 16th Duke of Norfolk and had a great affection for him. His Grace reciprocated in kind and when he died in 1975, having planned his own funeral, Chalky was asked to lead the funeral procession. In 1982 he was invited to a reception in St. James' Palace where the Marquess of Abergavenny introduced him personally to Her Majesty the Queen as "This is Chalky, my policeman!" He retired as a police constable in 1992 with more than thirty years' service and six commendations and lived in Goring-by-Sea. His hobbies included naval research, long-distance country walking, and gardening. Chalky White died in spring 2009.

The Naval Institute Press is the book-publishing arm of the U.S. Naval Institute, a private, nonprofit, membership society for sea service professionals and others who share an interest in naval and maritime affairs. Established in 1873 at the U.S. Naval Academy in Annapolis, Maryland, where its offices remain today, the Naval Institute has members worldwide.

Members of the Naval Institute support the education programs of the society and receive the influential monthly magazine *Proceedings* or the colorful bimonthly magazine *Naval History* and discounts on fine nautical prints and on ship and aircraft photos. They also have access to the transcripts of the Institute's Oral History Program and get discounted admission to any of the Institute-sponsored seminars offered around the country.

The Naval Institute's book-publishing program, begun in 1898 with basic guides to naval practices, has broadened its scope to include books of more general interest. Now the Naval Institute Press publishes about seventy titles each year, ranging from how-to books on boating and navigation to battle histories, biographies, ship and aircraft guides, and novels. Institute members receive significant discounts on the more than eight hundred Press books in print.

Full-time students are eligible for special half-price membership rates. Life memberships are also available.

For a free catalog describing Naval Institute Press books currently available, and for further information about joining the U.S. Naval Institute, please write to:

Member Services
U.S. NAVAL INSTITUTE
291 Wood Road
Annapolis, MD 21402-5034
Telephone: (800) 233-8764
Fax: (410) 571-1703
Web address: www.usni.org